THE ROAD TO UNITY IN PSYCHOANALYTIC THEORY

THE ROAD TO UNITY IN PSYCHOANALYTIC THEORY

Leo Rangell, M.D.

JASON ARONSON

Lanham • Boulder • New York • Toronto • Plymouth, UK

Published in the United States of America
by Jason Aronson
An imprint of Rowman & Littlefield Publishers, Inc.

A wholly owned subsidiary of
The Rowman & Littlefield Publishing Group, Inc.
4501 Forbes Boulevard, Suite 200, Lanham, Maryland 20706
www.rowmanlittlefield.com

Estover Road
Plymouth PL6 7PY
United Kingdom

British Library Cataloguing in Publication Information Available

Library of Congress Cataloging-in-Publication Data

Rangell, Leo.
The road to unity in psychoanalytic theory / Leo Rangell.
p. cm.
ISBN-13: 978-0-7657-0512-5 (cloth : alk. paper)
ISBN-10: 0-7657-0512-9 (cloth : alk. paper)
1. Psychoanalysis. 2. Psychoanalysis—History. I. Title.
[DNLM: 1. Psychoanalysis—history. 2. Dissent and Disputes—history. 3. History, 20th Century. WM 11.1 R196i 2006]
RC504.R362 2006
616.89'17—dc22 2006022771

Printed in the United States of America

∞™ The paper used in this publication meets the minimum requirements of American National Standard for Information Sciences—Permanence of Paper for Printed Library Materials, ANSI/NISO Z39.48-1992.

CONTENTS

The Trunk of the Psychoanalytical Tree Is the Freudian Theory of the Mind.

—Leo Rangell

1

THE TASK

PROLOGUE

Theory is not the thing anymore in the present ambience of the psychoanalytic world. The time was when theory is what held candidates and analysts together in an intellectual camaraderie that shared a larger bond in the background, the practical use of this mind-expanding game in the treatment of patients. After every scientific meeting, as the business meeting was going on inside, the younger audience would linger in the street or over coffee, arguing the differences between identification, introjection, and incorporation, or how far neutrality or anonymity extended, or whether narcissism per se was pathological or normal.

The conversations today are crisper and grimmer, and larger in scope. Are you a classical analyst or a self psychologist, a Freudian or a Kleinian, a Kleinian-Kleinian or a Freudian-Kleinian? Or a Kleinian-Freudian? The lines now separate people; they do not bind them. The most analysts ask for now is to be respected in their separate spaces.

As a broad statement, I will start out by stating that, in my view, the subject matter under study has, over time, invaded the instrument of study itself. The formulation of a major individual in the field, Otto Fenichel, who was at his peak in midcentury (his unparalleled, classic text was published in 1945), that "the subject matter, not the method, of psychoanalysis is irrational" (1945, 4) could not be adhered to under the growing complexity that ensued as psychoanalysis, because of its compelling and universally applicable content, spread over the thinking world. One might indeed expect such a dilution or contamination as inevitable under the workings of widespread large-group activity. The collective mind of the expanding group could not maintain that prerequisite. While the individual analyst could conceivably strive to achieve and maintain a consistently rational approach at least "well enough," to use a phrase common in the vernacular of psychoanalysis, passing the concepts of theory and technique back and forth among a large, actually worldwide population of analysts can hardly be expected to maintain a rational uniformity (or a uniform rationality). Rather, the method as well as the theory that spawned it have been compromised, coming to contain a variety of irrational elements within both, in the application of the method as well as in the theory itself (some would argue that what is rational should be under scrutiny; this will not be an easy treatise).

What was hoped to be a science of the mind has been overrun by social values belonging to communal and political life but not appropriate to the life of science. The sociological value of democracy has transformed the promising new scientific discipline that played a dominating role in the twentieth century into a splintered entity that elicits many reactions from the intellectual public, but not the respect and hope that it drew halfway into its hundred-year history. There are now many theories, and, to be politically correct, they are all considered equal. All of them are weakened and incomplete. None has strength or elicits confidence.

There were numerous streams of influence during the historical course of psychoanalysis that made for this countereffect, vitiating the breakthrough in man's creative thinking that offered a dazzling promise toward illuminating and ameliorating the "dark continent" in human life, the inability to understand, let alone influence, the many unpredictable permutations of mental life.

Sigmund Freud started out by learning how, as a human being, he could become an instrument of observation and deduction directed to the mind of another individual as the object of study. His effort, even as it met its initial success, quickly ran into interfering forces as the cumulating knowledge that resulted was to be shared, nurtured, and disseminated by other individuals, as was inevitable, progressing to increasingly large groups as the field took off. The interactions between many observing and reflecting human instruments could never be contained and controlled as could the independent activities of a few, or a small number.

If the individual struggled and worked at maintaining a rational stance in the face of increasingly complex data, the group had a more dubious time achieving such a collective state. It was not as if a microscope, or a telescope, or a celestial observatory, had been built and was standing there for any individual to use at any time. The observing instruments of many individuals were never the same, and however much they joined for a common purpose, they could hardly be expected to achieve unanimity, or, as it turns out, even harmony.

These obstacles were intrinsic to the field. But external circumstances and developments were no more hospitable to the continuous growth of a field that aimed at exposing revelations or insights that proved to be half unwanted and opposed. It should have been a harbinger of experiences to come that *The Interpretation of Dreams* sold only 351 copies in the first six years after its publication. Considering that its subject dealt with an emotionally meaningful experience of every person every day (the forgetting of dreams is part of the subject), this was a piece of history that needed to be explained.

This affective experience alone could easily have turned its young author off. But one of the traits of the exploring Sigmund Freud that I have always felt was of a defining nature was his ability to convert obstacles, even painful personal experience, into observable scientific data, so crucial in a field where subjectivity was itself the subject. Looking forward, this was the seed of his discovery of resistance, a nonpejorative finding, the defense against insight in a procedure aimed at it. The young explorer had first to overcome a hurt, a narcissistic resistance in himself, to see it. The scientific quest undertaken, to pursue an examination of the workings of the human mind, has always been met with a unique and specific ambivalence. Whether groups or individuals considering the field in general from the beginning, or individuals contemplating subjecting their own minds to the close introspection that was the new discovery, the prospect has always been met by a combination of interest, cooperation, and receptivity on one hand, and cynicism, skepticism, or outright opposition on the other.

Most of the present crisis of confidence being experienced by the field is usually attributed to external circumstances. There are many, and they cannot be minimized or overlooked. Among the external difficulties rightly pointed to are realistic economic factors such as the formidable time and monetary investments required; variable changing value systems; ecological changes in living styles and mores; and, in the modern world, competition by psychopharmacology, advances in neuroscience, and a preference for the quick fix, all of which have posed competitive paths. Not the least, obstructionism has also come from the historical advent of sociologic and philosophic postmodern deconstructionism, a general wave of antiscientific and anti-intellectual thought, applied in this case, as to many or all other cognitive achievements, to psychological issues and concepts.

Without minimizing the contributions of any of these external factors, I feel that a more important source of our intellectual decline has been a continuous inhibiting and erosive force within the field itself. This has been at its very ideational core, an undermining of the psychoanalytic theory of understanding the human mind. In my view, the most significant agent of this interior disarray has been the fragmentation produced by the various stages of theoretical pluralism. The steady march of new, competitive, and alternative theories, which had their origins at the very inception of the new discoveries, reached a more active, even a galloping, pace in the last decades of the century just passed. This theoretical multiplicity resulted, in my opinion, first in a spirited excitement, and then in a gradual disillusionment and demoralization, a gradual process that led to conflict, confusion, contradictions, and a fragmented whole. Both the coherence of the theory and the inspiration with which it came to be met and absorbed have been lost. I believe the two are related as cause and effect, that inspiration went the same route as a unified, coherent theory.

It is the course of this developing theory of the mind that will be the subject of study of this book. In the hundred-year history of psychoanalysis, the new science and therapeutic discipline reached a peak, suffered a decline, and has settled down to have its permanent role objectively assessed.

2

THE TOOL

THE BREAKTHROUGH OF PSYCHOANALYSIS

The breakthrough by psychoanalysis more than a century ago was over its theory of understanding. All that followed stemmed from that—therapy, applications, and the wide cultural absorption of its insights and discoveries.

Not all agree with this. To some of a more pragmatic bent, it is not the coherence or even the elegance of theory that elicits the interest and respect that psychoanalysis has achieved, but more simply the outcome. I am tempted to call this an American view—businesslike, practical, Missourian, "show me"—but this is also a universal node of appeal. While many, public and analysts alike, are less strict in requiring external demonstration of psychoanalytic results, others subject the procedure to the same expected rigor as utilized in the physical sciences, calling for empirical evidence. Some analysts, such as Wallerstein (1986) and Fonagy and others (Fonagy et al. 2001), have supplied such data, from which various conclusions can indeed be drawn, but many remain more sanguine, satisfied that results of this diffuse subjective experience cannot be quantified or otherwise meet the criteria of the more exact sciences.

As conflicts and dissension became characteristic of the field, with an accompanying decline of its standing in the family of science, its essential core, the central aim of resolving unconscious conflict, gradually waned, and understanding was superseded by a number of contiguous and changing goals. Parallel to outcome was outreach, the ability to affect public social need, thus to enlist a wider interest and support from without. With both of these, results take center stage, while the intellectual quality of the method shrinks. For both outcome and outreach, the importance of a coherent understanding ceases to be central. As the means of achieving this central goal recede, there is less concern about how the outcome comes about or what we are reaching outward with.

While many analysts who focus on the more practical aspects of the new discipline prefer to look at outcome as the main subject of excitement and interest, I believe that understanding has always been its primary appeal. Outcome without understanding would not have introduced a new profession into the world of science or intellect. More progress and promise, both for therapy and science, can come from understanding a failure than from experiencing success without understanding.

If outcome were the main appeal and the preoccupation by which to judge the psychoanalytic process, electric shock therapy, which produces more immediate and dramatic results, would attract more attention than any psychotherapy. The most direct approach to focus on outcome was indeed during the era of psychosurgery. In a recent biography of Walter Freeman, the father of lobotomy, El Hai (2005) describes Freeman's last refinement of the technique, transorbital craniotomy, in which a lobotomy is performed by inserting ice picks under the eyelids and pushing them through the orbital plate into the brain's frontal lobes. Performed on hundreds of chronic patients in the back wards of a state hospital, the procedure was ultimately performed on an outpatient basis. The anesthetic was one or two electric shock treatments. In a review of this book, Andrew Scull (2005), questioning the morality as well as the value of this approach, comments, "That these objections often came from Freudians, most of whose views contemporary biological psychiatry has consigned to the scrap heap, does not make them any less compelling."

CRISIS: PRESENT STATUS

It does not take this last-quoted assessment to document the present decline in the intellectual standing of psychoanalysis in the family of science. After a long, commanding presence, it is not a matter of debate that the discipline ends its century of dramatic dominance in an intellectual crisis, with both its theory and its method of therapy under siege. Viewing the current, universal ambience of psychoanalysis, our field is in a state of theoretical disarray.

Among modern or contemporary psychoanalysts, according to terminologies in use today, a mélange of combinations exists. In a scholarly book edited by C. S. Ellman (1998), a group of invited writers, covering the kaleidoscopic path from the classical ego psychologists of the mid-century to "The Modern Freudians," demonstrate how difficult it is to navigate these tortuous routes with any sense of clarity or coherence. The conglomerate "contemporary Freudians" today includes self-Freudians, Freudian-object-relationists, self-object-Freudian analysts, Kleinian Freudians, Freudian Kleinians, and other combinations.

Richards (2000), who makes a plea for civility among competing schools between which such chivalry is conspicuously absent, accepts the fact of rampant pluralism. "The world of psychoanalysis today is irrevocably pluralistic" (p. 12), and directs his efforts toward a hope for harmonious exchanges between the separate schools. He himself further divides contemporary Freudians into "ego psychologists, conflict theorists, defense analysts, and separation-individuation analysts," and developmentalists. He lists me as "a conflict theorist." Richards and Lynch (1998) in one of the fecund chapters in the Ellman book, include within their multiple developing groups contemporary ego psychologists, modern conflict theorists, and contemporary structuralists.

Perlman (2005) states there are some 150 psychoanalytic societies and institutes in New York State alone. Fonagy (2003) states that the "fragmentation euphemistically characterized in the literature as pluralism, could potentially be fatal to psychoanalysis" (p.15), and "The discipline ultimately faces theoretical entropy, with all writers jealously protecting their ever-diminishing psychoanalytic patch" (p.14).

Writing on the American's Openline in connection with my espousal of one unitary, total composite theory, some analysts (Richards, 2005a;

Hall, 2005; 2005), express the thought in various ways that each analyst has his own composite theory, that each selects and rejects what suits him/her. This, if it were so, would seem to leave little hope for a collective discipline. In a seminar to candidates, Grotstein (1981), commenting on the scientific status of psychoanalytic theory, stated that we should have a cafeteria of paradigms; some feel one for each analyst. A complementary view is in favor of a theory for each patient.

So, do we have ten thousand theories, or more?

Is it acceptable that a patient should turn out to have an Oedipal conflict or a problem with self-cohesion depending on which analyst he is with? How much confidence can we expect this to inspire? Or do we need, or indeed, as I feel we already have, a theory that will enable us to focus with more uniformity on what emerges from the patient? The bewildering challenge is to match a patient with an analyst. The saving grace is that these distinctions between analysts can be ignored in favor of criteria more enduring than labels.

A DEVELOPED FREUDIAN

I cannot say that I consider myself a member of any of the potpourri of categories listed above. There is no grouping with which I do not share some convictions, and none that I include myself in as a whole. Especially (and I think this will surprise many friends), I do not consider myself to be a "contemporary Freudian."

I look at myself more as a "developed Freudian"—that is, one who has retained insights and formulations that to me have endured over time and have proven indispensable, and who has added such new ones as I feel have earned inclusion.

I speak of psychoanalytic theory, not theories. In my view, there is a theory of psychoanalysis, and many nonpsychoanalytic theories.

I do not concur with the dire view that has come to be held quite widely about the irrelevance of psychoanalysis, nor with the extent or permanence of its decline. I feel that the contribution made by its basic discoveries has been at a fundamental level and of a magnitude that will remain an important part of the intellectual armamentarium of man.

3

THE DEVELOPMENT

DEVELOPMENT OF THE FIELD—AS WITH AN INDIVIDUAL

On the eve of the 150th anniversary of Freud's birth, I will address what I still consider the most crucial issue in determining the legacy of this latest major field of human knowledge: the fate of its body of theory. To help understand the current status and composition of the field, I will trace the longitudinal history of its theory in the same manner as is done with the analysis of an individual, studying its developmental course. The field of psychoanalysis will be on the couch, its modes of thinking and their accompanying feelings mutually influencing each other during the various stages of the course of its life. The century of psychoanalytic development will be under psychoanalytic scrutiny, tracing the conflict free periods of growth, the successive inevitable nodes of conflict, the compromise formations, those and all other final or at least current outcomes, the present status and state of health of the field, and its directions, tensions, modes of behavior, and external actions. My focus will be specifically on the progression and life history of psychoanalytic theory and the history of theoretical divisions. These are not the same as splits, which may or may not accompany schisms over theory.

EARLY FREUD—INITIAL UNITY

Freud started the path toward unification at the initial breakthrough of his discoveries. His earliest insights involved the confluence of phenomena heretofore disparate. Symptoms were seen to arise from the same base as dreams. Both were tied to character traits. Slips (1901) and jokes (1905b) came from the same source as more serious outcomes. Freud's self-analysis was in the same genre and stemmed from the same origins as that of his patients. The normal fused with the pathological. Findings from these specific discoveries all bridged to the psychology of mankind. Unity was the theme.

In this first round, the method that evolved, from which conclusions were drawn, consisted of observations (of free associations), theory formation, application of theory, further observations, more theory formation, and so on. The procedure and its aims were the closest one could reach to the scientific method applied to subjective data, by means as objective as is achievable, which cannot be without some degree of subjectivity.

Freud made of himself, a living human being, a registering scientific instrument, receiving data and evaluating them as best he could.

ENTER GROUP PSYCHOLOGY

Then came the group. With that, group psychology and group process were added to the mix. These altered the method of theoretical progression, which needed from then on to take this change of method into account.

To the scientific method just described, or at least the attempt to achieve this, an additional mélange of influences was added. As the theoretical structure being built shifted from the work of an individual to the consensus of a group, the inevitable inputs of group processes were added: group hierarchies, horizontal alliances, and vertical transference effects. The concept of transference was not yet known, but its operation was not thereby delayed. Moreover, the mechanism of transference displaced to theory, which I (1982) was to describe and add to the brew many years later, was operative from the start. Freud was at once a towering transference figure.

Freud found and usefully interacted with his early collaborators and had the same spectrum of experiences with them as we all come to have with our professional and social peers, which range from helpful to neutral to disturbing or destructive. Freud's early work was soon collaboratively assisted by the likes of Abraham, Jones, Sachs, Ferenczi, Eitingon, and others in and out of his "Secret Ring." But, not unlike groups in other endeavors throughout history to the present day, there were fallings-out along the way for myriad reasons. The attempt to establish an objective, experimental, scientific method to investigate a subjective, humanistic field, first by a single individual, then by a dyad, and then by larger groups as the science advanced, can hardly be unaffected by the need to achieve consensus in a group of three or more without adding significantly incremental complications due to the interpersonal interactions. Such influences during the course of psychoanalysis affected the course of further theory in both a confirmatory and an oppositional direction to Freud's initial efforts at formulating a theory.

EARLY MODELS FOR SPLITS

Freud's role with his colleagues has become a veritable biographical industry. But what he left with us to use and develop was a science about people, not one contaminated by them. Some of the early dissidents were models for what were to become known as splits. Jung, Adler, and Rank were the best examples. In each case, some segment of theory considered central and indispensable was contested or eliminated, and something less or not acceptable was substituted. Jung focused on the mystical and did not hew to the rational. Adler preferred mastery and power as central issues and frowned on drives such as sexuality. Rank pinpointed a new etiologic origin, at birth, but tended to downplay all that followed.

All three separated and went other ways, although not immediately. Rank was, for a time, the "favorite son" of the master, before the split between the two took place. And Freud made Jung the first president of the newly formed International Psychoanalytic Association before the rift between the two men came into the open. Early on, Adler walked out of the Vienna Psychoanalytic Society, and Freud wrote Jones that he was happy to see him go. I say that these differences were "models for splits," but these were not splits in themselves. The field had not yet been sufficiently developed for these ideological separations to have immediate organizational effects. Actually, the split nature of these separations came out in later years. Social work in the United States was surprisingly influenced by Rank, whose stamp was first taken over by the School of Social Work of the University of Pennsylvania. Jungian institutes were formed later throughout the world, and Adlerian groups as well, although in lesser numbers.

To the extent that all of these analysts incorporated some of the basic tenets of Freudian theory, such as the unconscious, repressed conflicts, the role of childhood traumata, and the theory of dreams, they remained within the family of psychoanalysis. Actually, in terms of what is happening currently, a century later, reconciliatory trends in process today are allowing for much amalgamation of the groups. Jung's nonrational, spiritual focus is finding a place today in traditional circles, with a good deal of openness to obscure, meditative, and other methods from Third World and various other peripheral sources, but not without being grafted onto the entire Freudian system that has since developed. Adler's theoretical points of emphasis fit today quite well into the system ego, but only as one of the three interacting structural systems. And Rank's work, if not made exclusive and overemphasized, would take its place in today's world in a series integrated with the works of Spitz, Mahler, Stern, and many others.

The fact that there were immediate separations was due to the rejection of the main original nuclei at a time when the contents of the new discipline were in their most formative stage, the borders had not been defined, and a stable state had not begun to be achieved. At the very start, it was what was omitted that was unacceptable, not what was offered, which would have actually needed to be considered, and in each case of which Freud went along for a while.

FREUD'S FIRST FORK IN THE ROAD

With regard to the early development of the Freudian trunk, Freud himself met a crossroads very soon in his path that was an exquisite challenge to his early methodology. Thinking suddenly about a puzzling, alternative explanation of one of his strong theoretical convictions, when Freud informed Fliess in a letter in 1897 that he now discovered that it may not have been actual seduction that was so universally responsible for his patients' neuroses but unconscious fantasies of having been seduced, he faced a major fork in the road. A challenge was posed to the rigor both of his thinking and of his character. Was the answer to be found in fact or in imagination—or both? Or should he give the whole thing up and leave, as Breuer did? Freud, of course, stayed and went on. But did he add unconscious fantasy to his earlier discovery of seduction trauma—or did he replace the old by the new?

I believe that after a momentary period of ambiguity and wonder, Freud went on to recognize a rational coexistence—that both applied and were in fact reciprocal, each influencing the other. But what is important for history is what the wider field did with this first significant dichotomy, which was to make this a source of perpetual unclarity. The vexing problem of nature-nurture, internal-external, never left the field of debate, providing fodder for strong opinions on opposite sides from then on. Applying to many future dilemmas, this became a node for a rampant ultimate fallacy of theoretical progression, to replace rather than to add. A new fact does not automatically wipe out an older one; both need to be assessed by objective criteria.

4

THE EARLY THEORY

EARLY PERIOD OF DISCOVERIES—THROUGH THE 1930S

Freud went on, with early associates, to build the scaffolding of the theory of psychoanalysis, constructing in half a century, until his death in 1939, a theoretical system encompassing human behavior that, according to Zilboorg (1941), was as comprehensive and coherent for mental life as had been accomplished for the human body in the previous two millennia.

The theoretical buildup was steady. To swoop over this majestic phase macroscopically, during this major fecund period, the new science/discipline grew upon a theoretical base that included, in its early stages, among many other conceptual building blocks, listed partially in sequence, (1) drives, dreams, the defense of repression, and the first theory of anxiety (from *The Interpretation of Dreams*, 1900); (2) psychic trauma, the superego, and the ego-ideal (in *Beyond the Pleasure Principle*, 1920); (3) *The Ego and the Id*, 1923; (4) the problem of anxiety (Freud's second theory of anxiety), 1926; and (5) *Five Metapsychological Points of View*, 1915. A sixth was later added by Rapaport and Gill in 1959: (6) group psychology, 1921.

Resistances were seen as data and led to defenses. This was a major insight, an achievement of Freud's related as much to his character as to brilliant cognitive skills. Freud succeeded in viewing obstacles as not being complications or deterrents, but findings. They were part of the reason we were there. The mission was to fashion an instrument that could understand a continuous, ongoing process, including the hurdles along the way. The goal was to keep a useful study going toward a total science of mental life. The Project, a more ambitious attempt to fuse the psychological with the neurological, which Freud (1895) worked on for a time, was put aside in the service of reality. Freud was also practical, and realistic.

THE FIRST TOTAL PSYCHOANALYTIC THEORY

This first cluster of theoretical propositions, together with many other contemporary explanatory essays, formed the first total, composite (Freudian) theory of psychoanalysis, the earliest formulation of a comprehensive theoretical system. There was no comparable total system built around any of the early competitive theories. Nor were any of the alternative theories built upon a parallel body of original clinical material on a par with Freud's "great case histories," or on other original clinical data; the others were purportedly derived from the same clinical base as Freud's.

Freud was not against change, to counter a common critique. His therapeutic method evolved over many early trials and replacements. His first theory of instincts, sexual and self-preservative, gave way to the second, sexual and aggressive. The first theory of anxiety, an early central formulation, was succeeded, or changed, to the second, equally central. Here, the same question arose: did he add or replace the first theory? In this area, Freud was articulate about his dilemma and verbalized his thoughts. The second applied, but the first could not be discarded. He was undecided. But there was a conclusion: "non liquet."

In 1955 and 1968, I offered a unitary theory of anxiety. Combining Freud's two theories, I suggested "now liquet." This was an early instance of my mode to cumulate, where I believe that both the old and the new continued to apply.

ENTROPY—THE SUBJECT OF STUDY ENCROACHES UPON THE METHOD

What I have described thus far was one stream of theoretical progression, the rational-scientific one. The other, a competitive path, personal-subjective-affective, that I described as making its appearance at once, was not to be temporary but defined a universal characteristic, of contest, division, and alternative directions, based on affects, not reason, present probably as early as men lived in groups. This was in fact the subject of *Totem and Taboo* (Freud 1913), the anthropology of individual incestual conflicts, which Freud traced as a mode of living back to the origins of man.

Limiting our interest to the development of psychoanalytic theory, progress proceeded along two parallel paths. One was the method of Freud's, assumed by his collaborators, each of whom became similar observers of data, undertaking to understand them, and joining in the expansions of theory that came from these observations—which, with increasing numbers, became increasingly confluent and cumulative. Alongside of this rational, scientific method was a path that was more affectively and subjectively directed. While the goal of the new science is to understand people—that is, for man to understand himself—it was also constructed *by* people. As such, beside Freud's demonstration that the rational could be achieved, the subjects of study, by a process of entropy, inevitably began to encroach upon the method itself. The Oedipal struggles, for example, the objects of study, could not be prevented from distorting the method being employed to explore it. Conflicts derivative of original families affect the work of analytic families as well. In this intense, new psychological group, theories and insights, their novel common object of focus, serve as displaced targets as well.

5

SPLITS

SECOND SERIES OF SPLITS—SULLIVAN-HORNEY: SOCIOPOLITICAL HISTORY

After the "presplits" of the pioneers and the laying down of a major system of thoughts came a steady series of break-offs over alternative, preferred centers of etiology. In the 1920s and 1930s, there came the Sullivanian (1953) interpersonal school. I link this to Horney (1937) of the 1930s and 1940s, focusing on the culture. Both were in keeping with mounting sociocultural conflicts of the time, pointing to a societal crisis that many saw coming. Both theoretical systems moved the center of the neuroses from the growing intrapsychic to the external world. External political reality and the mounting sociocultural conflicts of the time, rather than intrapsychic conflicts, became the primary causes of anxiety and neuroses in the new system. This theoretical change was the basis of what, this time, became the first official splits from the young American Psychoanalytical Association, which by now was a structured organization, its main role at this time being to define and preserve the young science of psychoanalysis.

During the turbulent 1930s, with increasingly dark political clouds hovering over the country and the world, a conflict began to face many students of neuro-psychiatry-psychology who were beginning to know and think about psychoanalysis. This was a dilemma affecting my generation of college, premedical, and other professional students, over Freud versus Marx in this time of ideological and practical crisis, as well as theoretical choices. While progressivism and antifascism were societal goals among intellectually progressive students, I came to feel, and made my choice, that Freud could explain Marx, but not the reverse. From my dawning understanding at that time, I felt that psychoanalysis could explain how economic problems fit into psychic conflicts, but Marxism could not account for mental conflicts completely in economic terms. There was much more in psychological symptoms than material frustration. This much I already came to know from my medical and neurological education and early exposure to patients.

As I look back, it was probably here that the political labels "liberal" and "conservative" began to be applied to the spectrum of believers in Freudian theory. Many, if not most, of those attracted to the mental health field, whether psychiatry, psychology, or social work, were of the progressive political spectrum. As theory began to present them with the workings of the intrapsychic, as opposed to or related to the external-cultural, decisions as to one or the other, or an amalgam of the two, needed to be made about occupational choice. Freud and Marx both had appeal. Consistent with my present as well as my past thinking, the theories and pragmatic philosophies of both writers applied to the problems of the day. But each explanatory system had its separate area of focus, one the psychological, the other the economic.

Those who chose Freud were considered by some progressives to have rejected Marx—that is, they were therefore conservative, or worse, right wing. Among the solutions, some made a choice of one to explain all. Many very left-wing individuals opposed, even ridiculed, Freud, assigning emotional problems as a whole to economic disparity. Some became Freudians and rejected Marx, being on the conservative side in their political views. And some retained both, with various compromises: Erich Fromm was psychoanalytic but socialistic. In general, neo-Freudianism was a solution that retained the dynamic in psychiatry-psychology and progressivism in political views. Sullivan and Horney were desirable solutions for this segment of psychodynamic thinkers.

For myself, in 1940, as I stood aside these dichotomies while contemplating occupational choice, along with a sparkling group of residents with whom I was surrounded, I had a positive reaction to both Freudian and Marxist theoretical views, although probably to both in an amateurish and simplistic manner. Facing patients with neurotic, not neurological, symptoms, while progressivism and antifascism were strong societal goals that I shared, I came to feel, and made my choice, that Freud could serve my professional goals without discarding my progressive political views. The reverse, however, was not true. Adherence to the sociopolitical program of Marx was not centrally relevant to the treatment of mental conflict. The latter was much broader in scope than linked only to external material frustration. This much I already felt from neurology and medicine.

Retrospectively, much has become known about a prominent group of psychoanalytic contributors who faced this same psychological-political dilemma at a higher level and in a much more urgent situation. This refers to Otto Fenichel and a group of analysts escaping and keeping a distance from the advancing Nazis in central Europe. The Rundbriefe (Reichmayr and Muhlleitner 1998), recently published between Otto Fenichel and all of this group, which included such analysts as Edith Jacobson and Wilhelm Reich, casts light on the poignant conflicts as well as solutions experienced by this group of progressive Marxist psychoanalysts, caught between their Freudian and Marxist beliefs and attachments. Fenichel, after a searing internal moral dilemma, also chose the psychoanalytic view as the ultimate superordinate explanatory system.

The forward development of psychoanalytic theory was much affected by this widespread intellectual dilemma. Returning to developments in this country still in the 1930s and to the younger group of new psychoanalysts at this time further away from the immediacy of the brewing disaster, for a large number who were politically tuned but not yet imbued with the fervor of the new science, the main emphasis came to center on sociopolitical pressures as the central, pressing stimuli to the heightened awareness of neurotic conflict. Was an intrapsychic focus to be pursued with such energy in the face of the major growing threats and traumata from without? To Horney, Sullivan, and a large group of progressive young medical and sociological students and early practitioners, their respect for and burning interest in external political reality affected their conceptualization of the internal mental world. To them, political, economic, and interpersonal problems, rather than intrapsychic conflicts, were the causes of anxiety and neuroses in the new, acutely aware, socially responsible ambience, however akin this was to the existential philosophy that preceded psychoanalysis.

This was the basis of what were now official splits, since these last two schools were almost from the start outside the main developing organization with its unambivalent internal focus. But to the same question that I have posed before, was this polarity—another example of the internal-external dichotomy—necessary or inevitable? In a formulation that I will employ throughout the entire course of the development of theory, I aver that the theoretical dichotomy upon which these separations were based was illogically and unnecessarily imposed. In my view, the theoretical dichotomy from which these divisions came about stems from another fallacy that has coursed through the history of psychoanalytic theory.

Here was an example of the second major fallacy to vex theoretical progress throughout the history of psychoanalysis, that of pars pro toto: a part is substituted for the whole. People, society, and the external world were used to crowding out drives, impulses, and motivations from within. The fact is that the main, evolving theoretical system always included the external world, and at its center was the world of people, our "objects." Drives are directed toward objects; they do not exist without them. People, and all other aspects of the outer world, contribute in a major way to internal conflicts. But selecting external determinants to the exclusion of drives, defenses, and the totality of intrapsychic dynamic events is to strip the new science of its substantive advances.

Freud himself, comparing Klein's work to Jung's in 1927, wrote to Jones, "All our apostates always grasped part of the truth and wanted to declare it as the whole truth" (Freud and Jones 1908–1939, 635). He had earlier said the same about Adler. "It is an almost universal human characteristic of these 'secessionist movements' that each of them takes hold of one fragment out of the wealth of themes in psycho-analysis and makes itself independent on the basis of this seizure" (Freud 1933, 143–44).

While the motivation of the new groups was social betterment, the intellectual dichotomy was artificial. The result, as with similar previous digressions, was inhibitory to the growth of a unified science. To add rather than replace, or to expand or modify while leaving intact what needs to remain, would lead to unity rather than division.

There was always, in my opinion, an unconscious knowledge of the illogical aspect of these chosen deflections. In many cases, enough of the new insights were retained—such as the role of the unconscious, of childhood trauma, and probably even of infantile sexuality—to stamp the dissidents as analytic. And in many cases efforts were overtly made to retain strong links to the main trunk. Clara Thompson (1950), for example, of the new interpersonal school, in a lecture series at the Washington School of Psychiatry and the White Institute in New York, attempted to note the points in common between the new current cultural theories and previous ones. In my opinion, however, she did not pinpoint the crux of the difficulty that was already beginning to make for the dissensions: namely, that it was not what the new theory *added*, but what each *left out* that made for controversy and isolation. The interpersonal is of course important, but is not also the intrapsychic? Culture certainly plays a part, but why not also the drives? Environmental factors are inescapable, but do they obviate an innate base?

1950—THE "GOOD" SPLITS

I entered the field of psychoanalysis in 1940.

Following training in neurology, I entered two psychiatric residencies and from there began training at the New York Psychoanalytic Institute. This was interrupted by the war. Following three and a half years of service in the U.S. Army Air Force, I arrived in Los Angeles in 1946.

With the exception of a book review I (1975c) wrote of the Freud letters, edited by McGuire, which brought that aspect of early history into vivid immediacy, what I have said thus far about events before the 1940s has been written from a distant, retrospective view. From midcentury, fifty years after the inception of the field, I have documented the history of the last sixty years from direct observation—oral history as it were—from the vantage point of a participant-observer.

To be sweepingly brief, after the end of World War II and its positive use of dynamic analytic psychiatry, and after the young analysts who had served in the military had resettled into their analytic communities, the next few years became a high point for psychoanalysis in social and professional life. Interest was general, esprit was high, candidates pressed for training, patients were many, and study and scholarship were valued and visible. With these numbers and this excitement, debate was everywhere. At this stage, analysts vied to define, utilize, and protect their product. While knit together as psychoanalysts, cleavages that had begun before the war, and the intense practice of analytic psychotherapy during the war years, began to create a rift as to the essences involved in psychoanalysis as compared to its derivative psychotherapy.

Events moved rapidly. The year 1950 was the apex of four major contemporaneous splits that defined the ambience of psychoanalysis nationally for the next two decades, through the 1950s and 1960s to about 1970. Los Angeles, New York, Philadelphia, and Washington-Baltimore each divided into two groups within a few years of each other. As with the "good" war that had just ended, these first definitive splits were regarded as "good" for rational reasons that could stand an open defense and discussion. The theoretical line of separation was, with slight variants, over the theories of Otto Fenichel versus Franz Alexander. The disputed ground was the analytic attitude; was it to be the corrective emotional experience as described by Alexander, or a neutral state administrating insights via interpretations, resulting in the patient gaining "freedom to choose"? While the controversy was over the technical method, it was not that theory was agreed upon. In my experience, the "new," neo-Freudian group in each locale, alongside its technical banner of supplying love and reassurance, also leaned, with respect to etiology, toward the external, cultural vis-à-vis the internal, biological, and early infantile. The peak of conflict and specific ambivalence was always toward the Oedipus complex.

This time the conflicts were within the main trunk, unlike previous break-off splits. Most of the current theoretical split was undercover as compared to the sharp division over technical precepts. Overtly, enough of the theory of childhood roots was officially retained to enable both ends of each pair to remain in the American Psychoanalytic Association under the shorthand phrase of "ego psychology." Yet in each pair, the "new" group leaned toward the "here and now," which was to become more emphasized in future developments, while the "older" group continued with the traditional reconstruction of the past. The older group in each pair was presumably more oriented toward the id, and the new group more to the ego.

Looking back at this stage from a later vantage point, we again see a false dichotomy. Even if the "corrective emotional experience," supplying what had been denied the patient in his development, was seen as an inconstant and insincere maneuver, was not the formal analytic attitude, which should have always meant objectivity *with* caring and fairness and decency, a new and corrective experience in itself for the adult neurotic, always suffering feelings of having been insufficiently understood? Alexander's technical analytic stance can be seen as a forerunner of the later "enactment," or even as supplying the "empathy" of future self psychology. Loewald (1960) was one who symbolized the retention of unity rather than a division into two or more. The classical attitude, as he wrote, did not preclude a new analytic relationship. The two are synchronous.

The classical analytic attitude was, or always should have been, both insight producing and corrective as a new model of understanding, tolerance, and fairness. Consistency of these traits, not changing analytic roles, was how this was achieved. Id and ego; infancy and Oedipal, and post-Oedipal; internal and external-cultural—only all together explain the summation of outcomes. But the splits were caused by ideas and people, not either alone, however much under the guise of protecting psychoanalysis. With the new groupings brought about by these organizational splits, and the modernity that "progress" demanded and wrought, rivalries and hostilities prevailed, resulting in the separation and splitting of analyst-friends.

6

THE GOLDEN ERA

1950s TO 1960s—THE GOLDEN ERA

The separate societies in local areas that resulted from this series of splits perhaps prevented more open divisiveness and enabled a sort of working unity. It was actually the partial separation, with the theoretical tensions kept largely muted, that resulted in all of the pairs, in contrast to previous splits, now living together nationally within the American Psychoanalytic Association (the American).

From the time of the "good" splits (considered good because of unclarity) until the next cracking open, to come twenty years later, harmony reigned under a theoretical truce. The American held both views together, with whatever strain was required, under the theoretical umbrella of the euphemistic "ego psychology." And it was this somewhat forced unity that was the background for the golden years of the 1950s and 1960s. To a lesser extent, this was a hidden replica of the administrative arrangements between the three groups in Great Britain.

Looking back, strictness of theory, along with humanity in treatment, was achieved in many individual cases—analysts on each side practiced the necessary rational amalgam—but not in the official credos of the separate societies. In each pair, one society in a city was considered liberal, and the other conservative; there was no thought of the necessary fusion. Even today, when these split societies are in the process of reuniting, these reunions are not on the basis of the rational construction of a total, fused theory. The mutual suspicions and recriminations remain; it is economic and pragmatic considerations that make for the mergers.

The American held both pairs, and the views of each, together, with whatever strain was required. However they lived locally, the representatives to the American, who were active members in each pair, met regularly at the American with friendship and mutual interests. With the social unity provided there, felt even by common membership for those who were never in person at the American, and the theoretical umbrella that bound them under the euphemistic "ego psychology," all played a part in producing a common bond among themselves and a unified front to the public. Unacknowledged was the incompleteness of each half alone, one without enough empathy, the other with not enough rigid spine. Also still in place were the differences, the identification with each position that kept the rivalries afresh. Under a false truce, with each theory needing something from the other, a fragile unity was maintained and held together "well enough." Intellectual interest remained high, spirits were exuberant, and patients abounded.

"Ego psychology" received its name with the perception that the ego was being developed and featured, where until then it had been the id. Here again, it was all or none, instead of both combined. Actually, there is no such thing as ego psychology. Neither of these structures constitutes a psychology on its own. There is no "drive" theory or "ego" theory alone, nor is there a separate superego theory. No theory of psychoanalysis, indeed no theory that purports to explain any human being, can rely on drives alone, or ego alone, or superego only, or the equivalents of these functions in other psychological systems of thought. I, for example, am not an "ego psychologist," although I am often automatically considered one. This widespread appellation is another of the common straw-men fallacies.

I am an id-ego-superego-internal-external-psychoanalyst-psychosynthesist. "Synthesist" because the purpose of psychoanalysis is not only to tease apart but also to put together. I have seen patients who have been subjects of analysis without synthesis. They were left in sorry states. I remember one candidate who was analyzed in a training analysis but was never synthesized, or put back together again. I saw him regress from an integrated and successful individual with some encapsulated neurotic traits into a decompensated person in a chronic anxiety state that spilled over into social situations and limited his ordinary adaptedness for the remainder of his life.

AMERICAN EGO PSYCHOLOGY: THE SECOND TOTAL COMPOSITE THEORY

The same correction belongs to the theory associated with the theory of the midcentury American. The theory that was central in the 1950s and was associated with the theoretical view of the American was not "ego psychology" as it was usually and loosely called. The appealing and dominant theory of that "golden period" was in fact the second total composite theory, the intermediate theory that had been accumulated and achieved at that stage of the progress of theory. Under this, there was at the time an operative theoretical unity, even as one that kept various disparate central emphases together. This was the Freudian theory amplified by developments since then, which consisted mainly of the catching up by the ego to what had been until that time mainly an uncovering of the id. Besides having from the start incorporated the object and the pre-Oedipal, both of which were later selected for emphasis in separate theories (Sullivanian and Kleinian), the total theory at this stage contained the pace-setting effects of Anna Freud's (1936) work on ego defenses and Hartmann's (1958) introduction of the adaptive aspects of the ego. Both of these amplified the scope of the analytic process to now incorporate normal, nonneurotic solutions and the conflict free, and to make of psychoanalysis a general psychology. In an obituary to Heinz Hartmann, I (1971) stated that in 1939, the year of Freud's death and of Hartmann's classic monograph, Freud had handed the baton to Hartmann on the top of a mountain, which Hartmann went on to build twice as high. While this might have been considered a lofty metaphor appropriate to the occasion, it could deservedly have been taken quite literally. Hartmann went on to do for the ego what Freud had done for the id. In this, he was joined by a worthy partner, David Rapaport in Topeka.

This theoretical development was coincident with the success of the American as the dominant spokesman for psychoanalysis in midcentury in the United States. Standing strong and unequivocally for what I now call a composite theory, embracing all elements that are quite universally accepted as enduring rather than topical, the American enjoyed its preeminent position as the ideational center of the mental health culture at the time of its greatest popular acceptance. It also held the fort in another connection—that is, internationally—coming to represent the antidote and contrast to the divisions taking place in Great Britain. In its overall equidistant stance, not just to the three structural systems but toward the entire span of life, this balanced theory represented to the rest of the analytic world the solid Freudian ground against the gaining system of Kleinian analysis, with its driven emphasis on one early etiological period of the developmental life cycle.

American "ego psychology," as the bulwark against Kleinianism in the International Psychoanalytical Association (the International) during the peak years of the 1950s and 1960s, was supported by leading medical and nonmedical analysts, and by traditional Europeans as much as by American leaders. I witnessed firsthand the affective bond between Anna Freud and Max Gitelson during the latter's presidency of the American in the mid-fifties, and of the International a decade later, as Ms. Freud and many other theoretical leaders who had emigrated here from central Europe lined up with American theory to contest the new, strong, divisive British view. It is well to keep this in mind in order not to conflate this theoretical position with the medical orientation of the American that was to generate much criticism and bitterness toward the Association, and which not infrequently was displaced to its theory.

7

THE CREST AND THE SLOPE: THE BREAKUP OF THEORY

END OF THE 1960s: THE CREST OF THE WAVE AND THE DOWNWARD TURN

These developments brought psychoanalysis past its first half-century mark. For two decades after the war, during the golden era in the American mainstream, where a theoretical surface unity reigned, the body of psychoanalysts, wherever they were clustered, attended with confidence the needs of an eager and enthusiastic patient population. This lasted to the middle or toward the end of the 1960s, when a downward slope began to come into view. I have documented, in an explicit account of personal and professional history, the forces that converged in bringing to an end this period of internal congeniality, and with this, the beginnings of a decline of the fortunes of psychoanalysis. Splits, I have pointed out, are caused by ideas and people. The combinations of the two that affected this still-young science were a unique and complex set of ideational and interpersonal struggles. I (2004) have described the latter in some depth elsewhere and will focus here on the ideational aspects.

After a period of strained togetherness over general theory and the basics of treatment, a more active set of divisive issues, of theory and technique, started in earnest in the late 1960s, coinciding with the onset of a decline from the psychoanalytic peak. I have described in depth the combination of scientific issues and interpersonal influences that went into determining the powerful directions taken by this course of our theoretical history. From this period into the 1970s and beyond, numerous successive movements gained popular followings, each objecting to and aiming to modify some aspect of analytic thinking or practice that was considered unnecessary or excessive.

Before smaller partial theories began, several large new trends occupied center stage, in quick order.

TOPEKA

The first of these major suggested reorientations was the developments in Topeka in the late 1960s around George Klein's (1973) question, "Two theories or one?" Psychoanalytic theory should properly be divided into two theories, ran the argument, a separate abstract and clinical theory. The former is abstract, speculative, and not supported by data; the second is concrete, direct, and based on observable facts. Besides stemming from close theoretical argument, over which one could agree or disagree, this new movement constituted a revolt against David Rapaport by a group of brilliant analyst-scholars who had been inspired by him over many years. This new view of G. Klein's was supported by Gill, Schafer, Holt, and others, who had been together in a close bond under their "inspirational Moses [who] discussed abstract metapsychology with the fervor of a political orator and the thunder of a Hebrew prophet" (Gill 1967, 5). One knows the fate of such prophets. They ask for trouble, and it is usually provided.

The suggested division now was within the main trunk, not a call for a split-off alternative system. The opposite of integration, this was a new way of looking at the total theory, and within that, at its main trunk, making it two, not one.

A counterview, linking to Freud's complementary series, had been expressed by Waelder (1962) that all theory is both clinical and abstract, some closer to one side, some to the other. Examples from clinical practice can be adduced at will. Transference, as an example, is a clinical phenomenon that is explained and encompassed by an abstract concept.

Abstract theory derives from and is connected to clinical observation, and clinical data are explained by abstract, intellectual thinking. One can in fact not be without the other. The two poles are joined by the complemental series described by Freud (1905a). Waelder's reasoning, however, had no limiting effect in deterring support of the suggested theoretical innovation. Dichotomy, polarization, and separateness were stressed instead of the continuity that often exists between seemingly opposite poles.

Here was another powerful example of flawed logic—in fact, not one but two mechanisms of looseness in logical thinking. One was the failure to extend insight gained in one area to another to which it also applies. Freud's contribution of the complementary series, offered in relation to gender and sexuality, made the revolutionary observation that sexual orientation exists on a continual spectrum, with variable degrees of combination existing between two poles. As theory developed, this mechanism could be seen to be operative in relation to many other seeming polarities, such as nature-nurture, neurosis and adaptation, psychoanalysis and dynamic psychotherapy, and many other dichotomies that from observations in life are seen as being joined by a graduated series of fusions and combinations. Clinical and abstract are such a joined pair.

The other flaw, applied to the same subject, is a denial of consequentiality. Rational argument, and the consequences of reason, need not be countered; they can be ignored. The spelling out of the fused nature of the seeming opposites, the fact that any observed instance is a combination of both, varying only in the ratio of one over the other, is not refuted but plays no part in the understanding of the assemblage of facts. Waelder's explanation has never, to my knowledge, been opposed or contradicted, yet it has had little effect. No change in opinion has been evident in those who go on to actively separate two forms of psychoanalytic understanding, a clinical theory and an abstract one, but do not consider that the latter is the explanation of the former. The fact that one does not exist without the other has no visible influence on those who hold this view. Rational argument can be easily overlooked. The mechanism of denial is a wide and profound one.

Shevrin (2003) has pointed out how the eclipse of Rapaport, as I can also add of Hartmann, and ultimately of Freud, and of the systematic abstract thinking that derives universally and constantly from observed data, has resulted in the gradual decline and ultimate absence of a comprehensive and coherent theory of psychoanalysis. It is precisely such an overall composite theory that I have suggested for years can be present if the analytic collective would embrace it.

LOS ANGELES

Almost at the same time, another intellectual, affective, and huge psychopolitical event was unfolding in Los Angeles that would go on to change the American theoretical landscape. As a result of considerable unrest and interpersonal strife, a window was opened for the entrance of Kleinian proponents and vocal emissaries to the Los Angeles analytic scene, the first in this country. In addition to the discontent with existing theory that is constantly behind innovations in thinking, this was brought about to a considerable degree by widespread dissatisfaction and interpersonal conflicts in an excited and charged emotional climate. Responding to invitations, there came to that society in rapid succession Hanna Segal, Herbert Rosenfeld, Betty Joseph, and others, followed soon by Wilfred Bion, around whom an equally excited nucleus formed and radiated influence for a while. What followed was a period of multiple theoretical divisions, cultlike groups, elitism, hierarchies, character assassinations of the old, and proselytizing for the new. As with the new and insistent emphases of the Kleinians, with Bion as well, there was no semblance of a complete system of thought, only views that were compelling to their respective audiences with sloganlike qualities. Yet solid followings took form toward each split-off theory, with separatism and intense devotion.

ROME—KOHUT

Practically at the same time as the turmoil in Los Angeles, and for overlapping interpersonal issues that I (2004) have described in depth, Kohut's (1971, 1977) self psychology made its appearance and met its receptive audience. I have elaborated on the connections of both of these events with political activities around the International Psychoanalytic Association's Rome Congress of 1969. Each theoretical development demonstrated the confluence of influences by ideas and people. In every major group upheaval around principles or beliefs, there is a convergence of the cognitive role of creative ideas and of the ways that these ideas are shaped and furthered by interpersonal friction and conflicts. For the broad influence that these events bring about, the human individuals involved are not confined to the leaders. The roles of people must include the contributions of and synergy between leaders and led. A significant movement cannot take place without the support of a group.

In Los Angeles, Kohut quickly replaced Klein and Bion in the Los Angeles Psychoanalytic Society that had brought them over, supported basically by the same shifting audience. The same followers moved quickly from Freud to Klein to Bion to Kohut, later to move as easily to object-relations and then to Stolorow. In the same city, the Southern California Society, previously neo-Freudian, post-Oedipal, and cultural, quickly joined the shifting new movements, opening up to Kleinian infancy and pre-Oedipal, later to the self, and later to objects. From a focus on latency and the external world back to infancy, the Oedipus was leapfrogged in both directions.

In the longer run, the Kleinians, rebuffed after being welcomed, went on to form their own society in Los Angeles with those converts who were more constant and consistent. The city went from two groups to many.

The mélange of theories that came to coexist, coupled with the affective force of the discussions, percolated up into the national scene. There, the sudden influx of multiple points of view was met by a receptive audience, for the same reasons as had been present in the city where the influx of alternative theories had started. Discontents with the existing milieu, for the same frustrations, disappointments with analysis, ambivalence toward the inevitable group hierarchies, and impatience with the slowness of progression toward analytic prestige, nurtured a growing sense of ennui and a desire for change.

Disaffected analysts are always ready to cluster around a new concept. An example of such a change in previous times that was not only readily acceptable but led to large groups of eager adherents was the wide cultural appeal of Erikson's ego identity in the 1950s and 1960s.

This was partly for valid reasons, in that it added to the inventory of ego functioning, but for many analysts, the new emphasis overshadowed and rendered obscure any accompanying intrapsychic determinants, which, for their affective preference, was the main gain. It was the same now with Klein, Bion, Kohut, and Greenberg and Mitchell. With both motives simultaneously involved, multiple vibrant and active new nuclei of analytic thought began to fall on receptive soil.

With the American beginning to suffer a decline in prestige, along with a dearth of candidates, increasing doubts about past theory were met by a burgeoning interest in the new. Issues of unity, or of coherence and consistency, receded, along with concern with the scientific method. In this regressive development, there was mutual cooperation between the leaders who formulated and the followers who accepted and joined, the apex and the base of the population pyramid. Followers of innovators were abundant and readily available. This was true within and outside of psychoanalysis—large groups ready to accept appealing concepts that were not wrong or inaccurate but incomplete, akin to Glover's (1955) inexact interpretations.

8

THE ASCENT OF PLURALISM

1987—THE MONTREAL CONGRESS

The mushrooming concept of theoretical diversity, already in motion, received a quasi-official stamp in Wallerstein's (1988) presidential address at the Montreal International Congress in 1987, in which he posed the question, "one psychoanalysis or many?" and supplied his own answer: many. Noting the multiplicity of theories extant at that time, Wallerstein stated that all have equal valence and validity. No one theory has the right by logic or performance to claim superordinacy over any other.

This endorsement of the eclectic position at the highest level ushered in a period of sanction for the pluralism that had been taking form. Greeted by a celebratory tone, the enthusiastic reception led quickly to its widespread adoption as almost automatic policy in institutes around the world, helping it to become the zeitgeist of the times. From that point on, the mainstream was no longer main. A small continuing opposition, disagreeing with this assessment, who preferred a central, inclusive theory that preserved the enduring Freudian points of view, added to by new developments in the cumulative manner I am espousing, were in the distinct minority.

Clinical theory, Wallerstein stated, bounded us together, while abstract theory separated analysts into competing factions. The former was direct, observable, replicable, subject to validation and deniability, and could be a subject of research, all of which were requirements of psychoanalysis as science. The abstract "metapsychologies," each theoretical system having its own version, were speculative and kept us apart. In support of these views, Wallerstein turned to the emphasis on the here and now over reconstructions and quoted the Sandlers' (1984) concept of the past and present unconscious as pointing in the same direction. The current, present clinical immersion is the common ground that analysts share, superseding the theories utilized as explanations. The past unconscious rests on the speculative ground of abstract theory. This view repeats George Klein's reasons for two theories postulated in the 1960s, extending it now to many theories, not two. Clinical theory, according to this view, is the common ground uniting all psychoanalytic viewpoints, making them equal and interchangeable, while abstract theories, which are speculative and unconfirmable, serve to separate them.

EGO PSYCHOLOGY AND THE AMERICAN PSYCHOANALYTIC ASSOCIATION

In follow-up conferences and subsequent writings aiming to further define the nature of common ground, Wallerstein went on to equate the American with mainstream "ego psychology," whose role he had questioned and diminished, and whose dominance he had just replaced. Singling out that association as the representative of that now-antiquated view, Wallerstein proceeded to denigrate the long theoretical stance of the American in contrast to the more diverse focus of the International. In this effort, he resorted frequently to the use of political terms, which in my opinion hardly fit the scientific issues. American "ego psychology," he wrote, was a monolithic hegemony (1991). My unified, total composite theory stemming from it was "imperialism by assertion" (1991). "The total, composite theory I advocate," Wallerstein (in Bergmann 2004) states, "grown by progressive accretion upon the work of Freud . . . Anna Freud, Heinz Hartmann, Otto Fenichel, and all the others . . . can of course be seen by the proponents of all other perspectives as an effort to maintain the one-time American imperialism that saw its own ego psychology as the only comprehensively whole psychoanalysis, with all the other theoretical schools as deviant or split-off partial positions" (209).

Actually, Wallerstein's own statement of equality of theories might qualify more for that description, having come about as it did as if by declaration. This turn is ironic by an author who in the past was himself at the center of the theory of the American, having served as its president in the early 1970s. In the 1960s in Topeka, rather than follow G. Klein away from Rapaport in his "Two Theories" paper, Wallerstein had remained with Shevrin and others who continued to support Rapaport's views. And until Anna Freud died in 1982, he, along with Sandler, were regularly the two chairmen and summarizers of the Hampstead symposia that spearheaded the same ego psychology that Anna Freud led in synchrony with the American. After Anna Freud's death, and as subsequent presidents of the International, both of these authors spread out to be inclusive of British and other alternative theories (Kleinian, object-relations, self psychology). To Green's (2005) assessment of Wallerstein's views as politically motivated (which would be understandable in the interest of achieving universal harmony), Wallerstein (2005) agreed that this was the case partially, the other part being scientific.

There is, however, another approach to the quest for harmony amid the conflicts faced within the field of psychoanalysis by an organizational psychoanalytic leader, as I know from experience. Democracy is hardly the method of resolving scientific questions. Equal rights do not mean equally right. Fusions, compromises, and choices among alternatives are other routes.

When I moved to the presidency of the International in 1969 after having held the same position in the American, both of which positions were also later held by Wallerstein, my scientific interest was to lead by comparing the two contrasting theoretical climates, to measure the total Freudian position of the American against the bipartitioned Freud-Klein division that characterized the International. My individual goal was probably not unlike the theoretical quest of the "Controversial Discussions" of the British Society thirty years before, to rationally compare and assess the contested issues and to decide upon or construct a rational fusion. In this, I felt I was at least partially successful, particularly in South America, where, during my years of activity within that region, I acquainted the primarily Kleinian analysts there with Freudian developmental and structural theory, and how, in my opinion, a total cumulative view encompassed the Kleinian pre-Oedipal aspects of development, merging them into the Freudian developmental line in a form that could be agreed upon by all.

In the meantime, coming back to the American, the new groups, formed during the tumultuous times I have just described, turned automatically to that association, where the prestige still resided. The American, until now the locus of "ego psychology," responding to the tenor of the times, gradually began to accept the multiple new pressures and to accommodate itself to the theoretical mix of the times. Now the American was changing. From the 1970s through the 1980s, the penetration of Klein, Bion, and Kohut, each claiming (by its large group of adherents) to be an alternative theory, added to by the continuing Alexander influence, challenged and changed the hitherto fairly unified theoretical atmosphere of the American, making for a more eclectic, multitheoretical consciousness. The American came more and more to resemble the International, to which, while still representing a fairly unified and coherent theory, it had until then served as a contrast.

The American Psychoanalytic Association has gone through various stages during the past psychoanalytic century. At this point in the successive developments I have described, it began to pass from the peak of its prestige to becoming the target of almost a paranoid hatred by the end of the century. After its formation and early development, which included at its inception almost an automatic, which proved to be fateful, decision to limit its membership to medical psychoanalysts, during "the golden era" at midcentury, the American enjoyed profound respect and was looked to as probably the best and strongest association in the psychoanalytic world. The International, more the scene of friction and discord, had been forced to negotiate compromises and to embrace discordant technical and educational arrangements in order to enable the warring factions to exist together. In contrast to the patchwork agreement that followed the aftermath of the Controversial Discussions in the British Society in the early 1940s, the American stood astride the various splits in this country during the first half of the century with a fairly comfortable stance, fortified by a uniform theory. The scientific position it had carved out for itself accrued to it the support and confidence of what had emerged as the mainstream of psychoanalytic thinking at the time of the greatest acceptance of psychoanalysis in its history. By the time the last quarter of the century approached, that ambience was gone. Along with that development, mainstream theory became no longer main and gradually turned into the defensive minority.

To continue the theoretical history that gradually brought about these evolving organizational and ecologic changes, I have thus far described the historical events that disturbed the stability of the theoretical stance confidently held by the American through the 1960s. From the 1970s, the increasing spread and influence of alternative theories—converging from the developments I have traced and resulting in the influx of Kleinian, Bionian, and middle-group object-relations theorists from the British—and the proliferation of self, relational, and intersubjective views within this country, all pressing from below and met with increasing receptivity from above, gradually eroded the unity of American theory. Until then, the American had been quite uniformly equated with "ego psychology." I have explained that this linguistic shorthand meant the total Freudian theoretical structure as built cumulatively to that time. By this appellation, the American was, in a practical way, the stronghold of Freudian theory vis-à-vis the main dissident theory of Melanie Klein, which co-existed with Freudian theory within the International as it did within the British Society and every region that emulated the British.

During its variegated history, in its strong phases as well as in controversial times, the American came to represent a number of pivotal positions that made it a target for intense affects. One important background mechanism that affected the image of the American throughout its history as the predominant organization, with the prestige that automatically came with that, was its being reacted to by a spectrum of displaced affects based upon the mechanism of "transference to theory." I (1982) described this as affecting all institutions, up to the national organization during the entire lifespan of analysts inside and outside the American. As the prestige and success of the American solidified during the first half of the century, so did its role and identification as the main superego figure or institution, with the displaced negative Oedipal onus that this brought about.

9

THE BAD AMERICAN

THE AMERICAN AND LAY ANALYSIS

In addition to these general group effects, however, there were, based on the prestige of institutional authority, strongly felt affects directed toward the American based on its stance on not one but several specific, highly charged, conflictful issues. Of the two strongest and most well known of these, one was its role in theory, just described, as the representative and main spokesman for Freudian ego psychology at the height of the century, as compared to the theoretical divisiveness more typical of and acceptable in the International Psychoanalytic Association. This firm position freely drew to it the authoritarian label. In addition to its association with "ego psychology," however, there was another parallel issue that provided permanent fuel for the denigration of the American that in my opinion is inappropriately fused and confused with the scientific subject of psychoanalytic theory. That was the long-smoldering question of lay analysis and the identification of the American with the medical requirement for psychoanalytic training. Probably the most divisive and disturbing long-term issue in the history of psychoanalysis, this wound at its center could not help but be connected in complex ways to scientific issues and to the intellectual status of psychoanalysis in America and the world. But this link also has dubious aspects—in particular, in my opinion, the claim of its relationship to the evolved pluralism of theory at the center of controversy about psychoanalytic theory today. I would like to discuss how this issue of training and turf affected the course of psychoanalytic theory, the roles that can be misconstrued, and where it is of relevance to the scientific status of the new social-scientific discipline.

The gradual negative affect toward the American on the basis of a unified, "monolithic" theory had a long-standing partner: the onus against the American built on the subject of its original medical requirement for psychoanalytic training. The "question of lay analysis" (Freud 1926b) has always been the nidus of controversy and affective reactions that have split analysts into opposing camps. Especially as the field gained currency and became a most desirable destination for a life journey and professional occupation, the criteria that became requirements for entry have acquired an intensity that inflamed passions. Practicing lay analysts, who had smarted under feelings of exclusion since the institution of the American's medical requirement, had for years formed independent study groups and societies. They had Freud's strong convictions to support them and had typically been engaged energetically for many years in serious scholarly studies that paralleled the courses of study and training in the American; in many instances, they were taught by the same individuals.

EGO PSYCHOLOGY AND LAY ANALYSIS—THE TWO ARE SEPARATE

These two charged issues, related by being foci of negativism directed toward the American, need to be kept apart. These two issues that split psychoanalysis—the scientific and the philosophic-administrative—have not always been kept sufficiently separate as to allow for clarity and understanding, to the detriment of a rational development of the field that encompassed both sets of practitioners. In the current theoretical ambience, this long-vexing issue of who can practice psychoanalysis, which carries with it a deep human and even moral aspect, tends to be adhered, for reasons of overlap in their developmental histories, to the subject of pluralism of theory. As both issues mounted in intensity during the same time period, the affect-laden and sharply divisive issue of who are to be trained as psychoanalysts, by being admixed with the subject of competitive explanatory theories, prevented a clear assessment of the fluctuating role of the American in scientific affairs.

There were overlapping areas of conflict in the two issues, in that both contained divisions between "insider" and "outsider," as described by Richards (1999) writing on the politics of exclusion. Richards considers the issue of exclusivity with regard to the question of lay analysis; I would extend the influence of this type of conflict to include the scientific arena as well. Within the institutes of the American, as well as in the institutes that had been kept outside, increasing resentment was felt by those who were "out" toward those who they felt were "in," but the object of resentment was different in the two situations. While to the lay analysts outside the American the onus for exclusion pointed to medical psychoanalysis, within the accepted institutes, to those who espoused competitive theories, it was the establishment's entrenched and arbitrary "mainstream theory" that was the target for feeling left out. In each case, the group that suffered exclusion felt the sense of mounting disappointment and cumulative frustration that Waelder (1967) pointed out is a common base of revolution, which finally comes to pass after a period of rising expectations.

The two issues became fused. A negative stance toward the American engendered by one issue was carried over to include the other. The experienced intransigence of the American on the medical requirement, drawing to the association an understandable and widely held criticism, led quite automatically, with less rationality, to the view of its theoretical position as authoritarian. From there, its scientific stance has been pointed to as responsible for opposite results, both rigidity of theory and theoretical fragmentation. While Wallerstein has spoken for many in pointing to the American's medical orientation as leading to a monolithic theory, Richards (2005b), also critical of the American on the issue of medical exclusivity, attributes to that same cause the opposite outcome of diversity of theory. "If more people were in our tent," Richards writes, "they would have learned from us and come closer to our way of thinking rather than go off their own deep end." While thus agreeing to the desirability of a unified theoretical tree, Richards himself has at other times, in the service of diversity of membership, been protective of the pluralistic view of theory as well. There is much confusion on the relationship between the two issues.

It is important to keep separate the subject of theoretical orientation from qualifications and standards for admission to training. The intense affective reactions directed toward the American on both scores calls for a close examination of each issue, which can lead to profitable insights on both fronts. Failure to do this blurs the line between the theory of psychoanalysis, or what the science is, and who is qualified to enter training to practice it, that is, the question of where psychoanalysis belongs in the family of science. Each question has its separate path and history. Theory can be uniform or diverse with either type of practitioner.

Empirically, in my experiences and direct observations, there is no correlation between having been excluded from the American and a proclivity away from Freudian or toward any version of non-Freudian theoretical belief. That organizational exclusivity and theoretical dissidence are unrelated is immediately obvious if one considers that Kohut, the most formidable deviationist in the American, was hardly an excluded analyst. Was Melanie Klein, the main alternative theorist in the rest of the world, excluded organizationally from the British Society or the International? Or was Wallerstein, the spokesman for pluralism, an outsider? Were not Wallerstein and Kohut presidents of the American, and Wallerstein of the International as well? Did these analysts "go off the deep end," as in Richard's offered opinion, or did they not have the support of and satisfy the opinions and affects of many adherents? And whether or not they were considered to have done that on their own, as it were, was such action related to their having been excluded from membership in the mainstream American or International organizational lives?

Yet it is no coincidence that the two issues, the pressures of discontent caused by the medical qualification and the opposition to theoretical unity brought about by the rapid advance of pluralism, are comingled. For one, the two overlap almost exactly in temporal contiguity. Both streams, equally charged, coalesced for a long time and came to a head at the same time. Wallerstein's "one theory" address was delivered in 1987 and published in 1988. The culminating lawsuit regarding practice was settled in favor of nonmedical psychoanalysis in 1988. A factor not unrelated to their fusion in the minds of many is the fact that the same person was a central figure in both subjects. Wallerstein, who was a strong force for the equality of diverse theories, was also a leading figure in bringing about the right to practice on a wider scale. It is understandable that the two influential activities of the same person should be received and reacted to together. It is unfortunate that one issue, universally applauded, was so close to and not sufficiently distinguished from another, questionable and controversial. With one role, Wallerstein's help in bringing about nonmedical eligibility, I am with the great majority in support; to the other issue, of theory and science, I am of the minority against and offer differences.

The arguments of the theoretical confluence of the two subjects, as I have shown above, come from two opposite directions. The intransigence of the American on the medical requirement is pointed to as a cause of theoretical fragmentation, while the same situation is pointed to as preventing theoretical diversity. Because of its isolation from the wider world of the International, Wallerstein (1998) writes, "The American could readily foster a monolithic hegemony of the ego-psychology metapsychological paradigm architected by Hartmann, Kris, Loewenstein, Eissler, Jacobson and a host of others" (560). At the same time, Richards (1999) states, "[The politics of exclusion] haunts us in the unabated fragmentation of psychoanalysis and in our lack of theoretical consensus" (12). Richards actually attributes to the American's policy of exclusiveness, which he traces back to A. A. Brill, both the dogma of ego psychology and the bane of pluralism. The shadow cast by Brill's politics of exclusion lingers to the present day, he writes. On the one hand, fragmented theory is attributed to that, and on the other, the deplorable penchant for dichotomous thinking, with the tendency on the part of orthodox practitioners to brand interpersonalists and others outside the institutional fold as "not analysts," can also be laid at Brill's door. Yet, to his credit, Richards also writes that Brill was indubitably a force for conservatism in the best sense. In a turbulent period, he "conserved" the science and profession of psychoanalysis against external threats and helped to create an organizational structure within which like-minded people could come together, learn from one another, and advance its frontiers. As a public spokesman, he represented his community with passion and commitment. Thus, although in some respects he furnishes a negative object lesson, Brill also suggests strategies for coping with—and mitigating—the divisions and disarray for which he himself bears considerable responsibility.

I believe that both trends, and the pervasive conflicts they have come to embody, are much larger than any individual and rest on the complex, ambivalent, and contradictory effects that the insights and propositions of psychoanalysis exert on the psychology of individuals and their derivative groups. They both welcome and reject these discoveries, simultaneously. From such forces, the theory is both supported and split apart. Brill, or any leader, plays the least part.

The fact that the long-festering, divisive question of lay analysis had a good deal of moral persuasion on its side, while the theoretical conflict was open to scientific disagreement, did not prevent the moral onus of one from accruing to the other. Wallerstein himself, by accusing the American on a moral basis for its scientific stance, probably contributed to this unfortunate merging. Insight into Wallerstein's own thinking and preoccupations during the late 1980s can be gleaned from his writings a decade later in defense of the role of the International in the notorious Cabernite affair in Rio. Responding to this, Wallerstein (1999) explained, "At the July 1985 Hamburg Congress, I was elected president of the IPA [International Psychoanalytical Association]. My four years in that office were in large measure occupied with the psychologists' lawsuit against the IPA and the American, an action filed in March 1985 and not settled until October 1988" (971). How difficult is it to believe that the solution of a conscientious leader to one issue spilled over and contributed to his attitude toward another, coexisting and equally pressing? Near the end of his term of office in the late 1980s, both confronting issues, the lawsuit for a wider entry into practice and the wide pressure of a profusion of theories, were treated with the same solution—the value of democracy—leading to espousal of equality in training, and along with it equality of theories.

To Green's (2005) challenge to Wallerstein, in a retrospective review years later, that his pluralism was a political decision, Wallerstein (2005) partially agreed. It was partially political and partially scientific, he stated; "I can agree that it was both; I feel that the two aims dovetail nicely" (633). It is true that a soothing harmony was achieved for the moment on the divisive issue of multiple theories, but more needs to be added. While fairness, intrinsic to democracy, needs to be maintained in human problems, democracy is not the mode of solution to conflicts in science. In the science and professional discipline of psychoanalysis, with its varied panoply of data, issues, and applications, a differentiating attitude is necessary toward specific problems and toward the particular aspect of psychoanalysis being addressed.

It would be well for theoretical clarity, for the esprit and working relationships of the large group of professional colleagues previously separated and now working together, and for the science of our common discipline, for the two parallel subjects, of theory and eligibility for training, to be examined separately. Multiple paths to training do not mean multiple theories; each issue contains its own criteria for evaluation. Both areas of tender conflicts have undergone different courses during their histories, and each requires a separate appraisal. While problems of training encompass both human and scientific issues, the approach to discordant theories requires an observance of the scientific method—that is, observational data and specificity of explanatory concepts. Scientific problems are not solved by popularity or by vote.

Regarding the taint on the American on these two scores, I would further consider the following. Beginning with the more modern era rather than the initial period of origin of the American, I would first counter the often automatic association of conservative with medical, and liberal with nonmedical and widely cultural, a misuse of politically tinged concepts away from their normal context. In this connection, I would point out that in two of the four definitive splits in institutes of the American around 1950, the "new," "liberal" split societies adopted the name of "Psychoanalytic Medicine," namely, Columbia in New York and the Southern California Psychoanalytic Society in Los Angeles. At the same time, most of the distinguished, nonmedical émigré analysts from abroad worked and almost always found homes in the classical, now "conservative," societies in their local regions, such as Ernst Kris in New York, Siegfried Bernfeld in San Francisco, the Katans in Cleveland, the Sterbas in Detroit, the Deutsches and Bibrings in Boston, Edith Buxbaum and Fritz Schmidl in Seattle, and many others.

In later years, when numbers were beginning to decline and candidates were sought after, both societies of "Psychoanalytic Medicine," Columbia in the East and Southern California in the West, quietly dropped the "Medicine" in their names and began to take leadership in training

PhDs and academics. Another phenomenon to be noted that is interestingly related, and usually overlooked, is that the American itself was internally divided, resulting in a national split, with the formation of the Academy of Psychoanalysis in 1956. In the new organization were those opposed to the "rigidities" of classical analysis, more culturally oriented in theory and more flexible in technique—that is, the "liberal" bloc. Ironically, however, a residual never made much of in public discourse is that while the American, the labeled "conservative" association, made room for special lay analysts, academics, and research analysts; was always a locus of ferment for the equality of lay analysis; and was finally opened up to the varied approaches, the "liberal" academy was, in its criteria for membership, at its origin and still today, limited to the MD degree. "The American Academy of Psychoanalysis and Dynamic Psychiatry is a national professional organization of medical psychoanalysts and dynamically oriented psychiatrists," says its current website. The American College of Psychoanalysts, founded in 1969, is also officially medical. Psychoanalysis lives under continual contradictions.

There is another historical decision that goes back to midcentury that can benefit from clarification: the separate regional status granted the American by the International in 1938. While this move is often referred to as a capitulation of the International to the medical requirement of the American, in reality the granting of this request, or more likely demand, was more to acquiesce to the American's insistence to regulate its own standards on a wider front. The dispute over standards for admission was accompanied by the beginning of a divergence of the two analytic centers in attitudes toward their common science. It was in the face of the American's beginning to consolidate Freudian theory, in contrast to the International, already well engaged in dividing it, that the American stood firm in insisting on its independence from the International in maintaining its own criteria and standards. The issue of separate status for the American, as recorded by Wallerstein (1998), came to a head in 1938, was deferred because of the impending war, became de facto in 1949, became formal in 1963, and lived on fully until 1987, when it was only partially rescinded because of the ongoing lawsuit about lay analysis. Only the rules concerning admission to training were then removed; other standards regarding education remained unchanged.

These others, I aver, were the standards regarding the science of psychoanalysis. While Wallerstein (1998) characterizes the American's opening up at that time to multiple theories from abroad—"British Kleinians, English object-relational, French (non-Lacanian as well as Lacanian)"—as converging into a new "richly diversified psychoanalytic landscape in the United States," one can take issue and consider the opposite about this "exciting reconceptualization on the American psychoanalytic scene." While Wallerstein attributes this widened view to the victory of nonmedical analysts, I (2004) have written in detail of the beginning of this theoretical sea change from the late 1960s on, two decades before the crucial 1988 legal decision and the overwhelming interpersonal factors around which these took place. Rather than being caused by any tension between medical and lay analysts, these changes affected both groups in the same and parallel ways.

The ego psychology that coalesced in the 1950s and 1960s within the American separated it from the theoretical center in Britain, exported throughout the Continent, as a frontline defense of the Freudian theoretical system, experienced in America at the time as against the interpersonal and cultural schools at home and the growing Kleinian school abroad. It was this theoretical role, combined with its medical orientation, that made for the American's sensitivity to retain its own criteria. I remember firsthand the affective closeness between Max Gitelson and Anna Freud after the war, Ms. Freud feeling much closer to the American ambience of that period than to the British or International. Gitelson was for many a symbol of disagreement with Franz Alexander in the American and with Melanie Klein in the International. The separate status of regional association, giving the right to control its own standards to the American by the International in 1938, stood as much for its scientific stance as for its medical orientation. The American "ego psychology" of midcentury (shorthand for total Freudian theory) was the major home of Freudian as opposed to the Freudian-Kleinian-object-relational scientific orientation in England and the International at the time.

After years of separate paths in this country, between Freudian, Kleinian-Sullivanian, and other divergent theories, before the major lawsuit over the nonmedical issue in the 1980s, the first threat of a lawsuit was not over lay analysis but arose after the Kleinian invasion in Los Angeles, when Susannah Isaacs, a respected British Kleinian analyst, and MD, was being rejected for membership in the Los Angeles Psychoanalytic Society of the American in 1975. After much to and fro involving both the American and the IPA, to whom Isaacs had complained, the American stepped aside from the conflict, and Isaacs was granted membership some years after she had returned to England. The medical degree was obviously not the issue. The American avoided a showdown as to whether it had a legal right to define and maintain its intellectual base.

Political criteria have not failed to play a major role in discourse over theory. Pluralism and eclecticism are quite universal in institutes today in the service of equality of theories. This has superseded the scientific method of observation-theorizing-testing and seeking consensus. The American, from the 1970s on, partly in response to realistic external pressures, was less firm in continuing its scientific position and abdicated its right to define and maintain its intellectual spine, the total theoretical system around which it was based. This is a compromise that has exerted a price. While democracy is relevant in general group issues, it is hardly the arbiter in science.

To continue to examine the role of the American, to understand more carefully and in depth how the crucial decision came about that introduced the deep cut in American training paths, the fact is that this division of the participants into two separate factions did not take place in a vacuum. Nor did this very disturbing dichotomy occur necessarily for reasons of selfishness, arrogance, or protection of turf, or at least not for an aggregate of such reasons without a mixture of more socially acceptable and other deeply determining motives. While this is still a tender subject even to discuss, in the face of the accumulated bruised feelings of a large population of dedicated professionals long practicing an important and needed profession, attendance to the facts of history might still be useful for a rational appraisal. This divisive event, searingly painful as it has been, occurred against a complex historical background and should not be the sole criterion by which the American is judged in this century of organizational life and strife.

10

THE PROBLEM OF LAY ANALYSIS

PLURALISM AND LAY ANALYSIS

To examine historically the relationship within psychoanalysis between the paths of origin of its early practitioners and their differences in attitude toward theory, adherence to Freud's developing theory was from the beginning in no way correlated with the professional orientation of his early band of followers. For an Abraham or Jones, who were behind Freud, there were Adler and Jung against him. All were physicians. Ferenczi, who was a neurologist, as was Freud, and Rank, an artist, probably the first lay analyst, coauthored a book on technique. A physician and an artist, each of them had biphasic relations, not synchronously, with Freud. Fliess was an ear, nose, and throat physician, far from Freud's neurology. Freud's ring mixed medical and nonmedical analysts. In a later era, Sullivan, looking to objects rather than drives, and Horney, who stressed culture, two early American dissidents, were both physicians; Erich Fromm was not. Melanie Klein, probably the most influential dissident theorist, never attended a university, yet one of her most controversial concepts, on aggression and the death instinct, bordered on the biological. Waelder, who represented the Viennese Freudian position in debates against the British Kleinian theorists, was nonmedical, a physicist.

Theories and degrees remained unrelated through future history as well. Anna Freud, Erik Erikson, and Ernst Kris were lay analysts, strongly allied with American ego psychology. Jones, a physician, was first closest to Freud, and then a supporter of Klein. More contemporarily, Kohut, an MD, a strong Freudian for much of his career, became a Kohutian later in his journey, in 1969, in part, if not largely, for reasons far from scientific (Rangell 2004). Classical contributions were made by Hartmann, a physician; Anna Freud, an educator; and Waelder, a physicist. Divergent or alternative theories have been proposed by Kohut, a physician; Rank, an artist; and Stolorow, a psychologist.

Among those who attribute much of present-day unclarity to the long period of strife between the two main separated groups of lay and medical practitioners, there are assertions in opposite directions. To Wallerstein (1998), the policy of the American to exclude lay analysts led to the dominant "hegemony" of American ego psychology, with its inhibition of the development of other democratically formed alternative theories. Richards (1999), however, attributes to the same exclusionary policy the opposite effect, holding this long state of affairs responsible for the multifaceted array of theories in place today. In line with his holding one man mainly responsible for this direction, he states, "It cannot be denied that the dark side of Brill's legacy bears no small measure of responsibility for the travails of pluralism" (2).

I agree neither with Wallerstein (1998), who attributes the "hegemony" of American ego psychology to its policy of having excluded lay analysts, nor with the opposing view of Richards (1999), who attributes the array of theories to the same exclusionary policy. Rather, each group contains within it a mixture of individuals who favor one view or the other. Ironically, each of these two authors has also had feelings opposite to what is now expressed, Wallerstein having once been a prominent American ego psychologist, and Richards at times defending pluralism as an indication of democracy.

In my observations and experience, there is no empirical correlation between exclusion from the American and any proclivity away from Freudian or toward any version of non-Freudian theoretical beliefs. Empirically, from direct contacts with groups around the world, I have found no correlation between eclectic theoretical beliefs and medical versus nonmedical training paths. Independent societies, some with long histories before the lawsuit, went through the same phases and divisions as American psychoanalytic institutes did, with the same proportions of analysts holding traditional and dissident theoretical beliefs. In my scientific and educational capacities, I have addressed many such predominantly nonmedical psychoanalytic groups during the years. I was struck by how much the scientific course of these parallel groups and institutions had come to resemble that of the main bodies. Sharing as they did the same profession, the same literature, and the same clinical data, it is not surprising that the history and development of their theoretical views should have overlapped. Lay and medical psychoanalysis seemed to have progressed along parallel paths, influencing each other in their intellectual preferences and beliefs, and reflecting the same processes of partly retaining classical concepts and partly replacing them with multiple schools of theoretical dissension.

It is as true now as it was in the beginning that it is not the division between medical and lay analysts that makes for dividing lines within theory, but the division between those who support the essence of Freudian theory and those who obstruct it. It was the independent New York Freudian Society, not the medical American, who were the main hosts for my unitary Freudian theory in 1996. The two polarities to which our present essay has led, the medical/lay division and the question of unity versus pluralism of theory, have in my opinion a random relationship without an overlapping connection between them. The conclusion I have come to is that the enduring theory is not related to paths of entry. Analysts coming from any discipline can for many reasons go many ways. Disagreements and alternative theories arise from the same complex reasons, cognitive and affective, related in part to diverging interpretations of observable data, but equally to hierarchic interpersonal relations. Disappointments in analysis or in analytic societies can lead to theory change in any direction. Scientific issues, in my experience, have not been the dominant causes of theoretical change.

My experience does not bear out the statements of Schneider and Desmond (1994), writing about the lawsuit for Division 39, of the connection between the process of exclusion and stultification of scholarship and creative contributions to mainstream psychoanalysis. The "golden years" of theory and practice existed in the very midcentury that the separation of practitioners was in place, and contributions to mainstream and dissident theories came from both medical and non-medical analysts, with no particular preponderance of one over the other. I also would question their quote of Jacoby (1986) about the American attitude toward European émigré analysts "in effect limiting psychoanalysis' scholarly tradition while elevating its practice function" (314). I entered the field in that period. Scholarship was at its height, and the European analysts were in the thick of it. Erickson was beginning to be read as much as Hartmann. They were, as a group, inspiring to the incoming generation, and I remember many of them as in the full bloom of their creativity.

Nonmedical, as well as medical, analysts were active contributors, leaders, and advocates on both sides of Freudian theory. The displaced European émigrés in each city, a variable combination of lay and medical analysts, were mostly the classical nuclei around whom traditions continued. But Melanie Klein was also a nonmedical analyst, and the pioneer of the most significant alternative to Freud ultimately around the world. Further, neither the quantity nor the quality of scientific contributions, nor the ratio of Freudian to divergent theories, nor the relative emphasis between clinical and applied contributions changed perceptibly after inclusiveness was effected. To be sure, there was a spurt in liveliness throughout the profession by the large, enthusiastic, and energized influx. But I believe that the diminishing unity and coherence of theory, in relation to pluralism, splitting, fragmentation, and increased inconsistency, resumed its course and continued as before. Both arms of the discipline, medical and nonmedical, have contributed to and distracted from the forward course of theory. Both share responsibility for the integrity and the defects of its theory.

11

THE PROBLEM OF MEDICAL ANALYSIS

THE ROAD TO THE MEDICAL DECISION

If unfamiliarity, or at least lack of expertise, with the body is considered a drawback in the clinical background of the nonmedical analyst, a parallel concern held by many about the counterpart medical analyst could be a distant relationship to the spirit of the patient. That an analyst who is also a physician is likely to share with medicine a cool relationship to the mind of the patient, to think of the patient as a structure and to relate to the mind as a brain, is partially true, but only partially true. And to the extent that the present era continues to be "the year," or years, "of the brain," many lay analysts are also looking that way.

But need it be that way? It is not without reason that Neutzel (2005), in a recent appraisal of the "the soul of our Association," wrote, "The American Psychoanalytic Association has a long and proud history. Founded in an era of reform for medical education in the early part of the 20th century, the Association assumed a medical psychoanalytic identity. High quality and thorough psychoanalytic education has been a central focus of the Association from its inception" (5). Although it attached itself at its outset to medicine, by introducing and standing for a strong edifice of psychoanalysis, it infused into the medical field the soul of the patient.

Yet the decision of the American for a medical identity created the most significant split in the field, and poignantly the only one that did not overtly center around a difference in theory. Nor was it called or thought of as a split, perhaps for that very reason. I believe it will be useful, in the service of understanding and hopefully of healing, to take a more detailed look at the surrounding milieu at the time of the birth of the American as it embarked upon its conflictful course—as well as at many complex, biphasic events since then. The identity of the American as a medical organization is also only partly accurate. It is well to look at its history in greater depth.

The American Psychoanalytic Association was founded in Baltimore on May 9, 1911, by James J. Putnam, president; Ernest Jones, secretary; A. A. Brill; Stanley Hall; Adolf Meyer; Smith Ely Jelliffe; William A. White; and eight others. To explain the fateful orientation that followed and the almost automatic confluence of the new healing profession with the medical field, Richards (1999) has focused on the influence and motivations of one man, A. A. Brill, as an ambitious immigrant Jew courting the medical profession, and the effect he exerted on the development of psychoanalysis under the aegis of the medical profession. I would have us look at a wider cultural influence and determinant than the power and influence of an individual. This is in keeping with my (1975b, 1976, 1980, 1981a, 2004) shifting the attention in much of large-group behavior from leaders to led, from the tip to the base of the population pyramid. Most large-group effects cannot take place without the compliance or even more active participation of the general involved populace.

One year before the founding and first meeting of the American Psychoanalytic Association, the American medical education system had received the results of a blue-ribbon, revolutionary investigation into the scattered, unscientific, and uncontrolled status of American medicine up to that time, culminating in the widely respected Flexner report (1910) on the status of medical education. At the turn of the twentieth century, physicians in America varied tremendously in medical knowledge, therapeutic philosophies, and aptitudes for healing the sick. Teaching and training methods were chaotic, followed no standard, and were often by private apprenticeship. Throughout the second half of the nineteenth century, there was hardly any regulation or standardization of medical education, because political traditions in America dissuaded national regulation of professions and because the American public and much of the medical profession were not convinced that any particular brand of medical education was significantly superior to any other (Beck 2004). Osteopathic, homeopathic, chiropractic, and eclectic positions commanded equal value; there was no superior, established scientific position.

But there was also in progress a movement toward rationality and science. By the turn of the century, a series of scientific breakthroughs had exposed the irrationality of many such widely accepted treatments as blistering, bleeding, and purging, and had proven the therapeutic efficacy and rational scientific basis of modern practices, such as antiseptic surgery, vaccination, and public sanitation. Most of the public and virtually all physicians were beginning to believe in the scientific approach, while educators at leading medical schools now stood for the systematic application of the scientific method. Direct observations, laboratory experimentation, and hands-on care were increasingly the respected mode.

Under these undulating conditions, the Council on Medical Education, created by the American Medical Association (AMA) to promote the restructuring of U.S. medical education, undertook a survey of medical education in the United States to promote a reformist agenda. Backed by the Carnegie Foundation, the respected educational theorist and social reformer Abraham Flexner, who had started and was the first director of the famed Institute for Advanced Study at Princeton, was chosen to head this survey. By standardizing curricula and training methods, this was to revolutionize the state of medicine and set the stage for a pervasive scientific attitude in the healing professions. The influential report that emerged concluded, "If the sick are to reap the full benefit of recent progress in medicine, a more uniformly arduous and expensive medical education is demanded."

It was against this background that the revolutionary insights discovered in Vienna and then brought to this country by Brill in the first decade of the new century, and by Freud and his entourage directly in 1909, became the contents of the new American Psychoanalytic Association in 1911 and merged quite automatically into American medicine. This linkage was not firm in the first decades, as the American association was not yet structured or organized, and the discipline itself was not as fully appreciated or valued as it was to become. Early standards and practice were loose and quite unregulated, as the future of the field was hardly heralded and did not have a flock of adherents in its early stages. It was not until the mid-thirties—under pressure from the New York County Medical Association, which, reacting to some glaring abuses in medical practice, had outlawed the practice of medicine by anyone not registered as a medical doctor and involved in public health—that first the New York Psychoanalytic Institute, and then the American Psychoanalytic Association, established the official policy that training for the path of psychoanalysis would be exclusively limited to psychiatric residents.

The road to an official, organized psychiatry, as to medicine, also followed from long historical antecedents. Long before the problem confronted the new American Psychoanalytic Association as to where and how to include the new mental discoveries, psychiatry, the science and the practice of treating mental illness, had embraced, or accepted, mental symptoms within the organic nervous system, and thereby into the medical fold. In a two- to three-hundred-year history, moving slowly toward humanism and democracy, attitudes toward the mentally ill had traversed the path from Weyer, at the end of the sixteenth century, in the first psychiatric revolution, effecting a change from witchcraft and demonology toward humanism and a natural—that is, observational—look at man; to Pinel at the turn from the eighteenth to the nineteenth century, freeing the mentally ill of their chains and changing their status from inmates to patients; to Benjamin Rush and Dorothea Dix in the mid-nineteenth century in this country, and their roles toward an American psychiatry; to the Kraepelinian age of systems at the end of the nineteenth century; to the second (Freudian) revolution at the end of that century, moving from psychoses to the neuroses and more normal pathology, changing the locus and methods of psychopathology from the organic neurological to the functional sphere. A whole new world of origins came into view. While the brain, or various parts of it, might still be the loci and the pathways for the observed phenomena, the mind, or ideas and affects experienced and communicated, entered the field of scientific data and challenge. There was now no physical cause (though there may be a cerebral accompaniment) of malfunction, but a causative idea.

For the nascent American, it was not much of a leap to include this new extension under medicine, and under psychiatry. Anywhere else would have needed much more explanation. The new mental was in fact modeled after somatic pathology, even if not within it. Zilboorg (1941), the premier historian of medical psychology, sums up the Freudian revolution as achieving the same type of specificity with regard to mental illness, the relationship of repressed traumatic memories to specific symptoms and psychopathology, as Koch, Pasteur, and the microbe hunters had discovered for bacteriology and somatic disease the century before. While, viewed from further experience, this may have been an optimistic appraisal, the broad outlines had validity. Coupled with the zeal of the times toward institutional reform, the ascendancy of science, and the role of prevention and public health, the new leap forward belonged in the medical field, as perceived at that time by serious scientists, notwithstanding the contrary view of Freud. And Freud himself was zealous to achieve scientific status and acceptance for the new discipline.

The designation of the medical label for the new discipline by the original American was not as arbitrary or as automatically due to considerations of turf or an arrogant hierarchy as has been commonly thought, or even a manifestation of the American character as compared to the European, an opinion in line with Freud's feeling about the fate of his discoveries to be expected in America, but was due to much more subtle and complex considerations. The link was quite natural. Two serendipitous facts planted the new science within medicine, one that Freud was a physician, and the other that the discovery of psychoanalysis and its first insights were made in the course of conducting therapy. It was as a neurologist, a physician, a healer of symptoms, that Freud first suggested free associations as a method of cure for patients' complaints. His evidence was from the clinical realm, his data case histories. As he first exposed his new ground, and rebuffs were his common initial experiences, Freud coveted the recognition and approval of the medical field. He aspired to teach in the University of Vienna Medical School. He sought respectability and was wary of wild analysis. All of this was background for his work's being accepted in America under the rubric of medicine. There was no reason to feel disappointed, only every reason to feel vindicated. The acceptance of the new discoveries into the newly reformed and regulated medical world in this country could have been considered a coup for the new profession, by no means yet established as belonging to the family of science.

Yet Freud himself resisted making this connection the decisive one. There was a wider and deeper insight to be mined from the new explorations that was truly beyond medicine. Freud did not come out with his widely accepted and much-quoted assertion as to where psychoanalysis belonged until 1926, some years after the origins, only after there had been years of accumulated practice and after more experiences and their implications had been intellectually digested. Only after many cumulative hours of free associations were the larger social implications of the new science beginning to dawn on the populace. While clinical was the base, society could be the recipient.

In 1926, in a poignant yet sharp piece of scientific writing, Freud dealt with this subject in depth when he intervened in the prosecution of Theodore Reik by the Austrian government for "quackery," that is, treating a patient without a medical degree. Here, Freud asserted that psychoanalysis could not be swallowed up by medicine or psychiatry and that being a "layman" in psychoanalysis was not related to the doctor of medicine degree but to the question of proper training for the practice of psychoanalysis. His (1927) conclusion was unequivocal: however definitively the psyche was rooted in brain structures and cerebral processes, the mind that emerged was a branch of psychology; "psychoanalysis is not a particular branch of medicine. I do not see how anyone can refuse to recognize this. Psycho-analysis is part of psychology—not even of medical psychology in the old sense of the term, or of the psychology of morbid processes, but, simply, of psychology" (393). When Freud brought psychoanalysis to America in 1909, it was to psychology, not psychiatry; his invitation came from G. Stanley Hall, one of the founders of the American Psychological Association.

I venture an interesting connection. The year 1926 was also the year of publication of Freud's revised theory of anxiety, a work I consider second in importance for theory only to *The Interpretation of Dreams*. In my own version (1955a, 1968) of the fusion of Freud's two theories of anxiety, I pointed out that the second theory, of anxiety being the signal of danger, was psychological, hermeneutic, and related to meaning, while the first theory was at its base physiological and mechanistic, a process of increasing tension, of cumulating, undischarged libido and/or aggression spilling over and progressing to cause anxiety. I (1963a, 1963b) also demonstrated, via the steps of "the intrapsychic process," in contrast to theories of Waelder and Brenner, that both theories continue to apply, that Freud did not abandon his original theory of anxiety. I here suggest that the first anxiety theory linked Freud to medicine and physiology, to the body, which Freud always felt was at the base, while the second solidified the link to the world of meaning, to hermeneutics, to psychology. The earlier theory of dreams had introduced both aspects together. The field belongs to both the somatic and the derivative psychological. Both apply permanently.

It was under the sway of this development that Freud distanced himself from medicine and decisively embraced the wider world of culture.

NEUROSCIENCE—A RETURN TO NEUROLOGY, OR THE ADDITION OF A LOCUS?

The latest turn of the science, a period of great interest in the field of neuroscience, brings the subject back full circle to the neurology from which it started. The relation between the brain and the mind has continued to occupy the interest of a multitude of analysts and neuroscientists over the years, and has returned with renewed activity and findings in the most recent period. But while advances at this interface have indeed been impressive, and many look to this area for new explanatory power, these have not yet achieved a form usable for psychoanalytic or even neurological purposes. Here, too, as with other areas of new focus and attention, perspective is necessary to counteract excessive expectations. Although the new links between cerebral visualization studies and mental processes are exciting and promising, their scientific value has not been clearly established. There has by no means been any definitive determination of how much the organic "causes" the mental, or the behavioral the somatic. We do not yet know to what extent the two are causal or correlative or what other qualitative mechanisms might influence their association.

The same principle of complementariness applies to this latest turn to neuroscience as with other valid and promising discoveries. Neuroscience, the latest area of insight (and of potential false exclusivity), provides one of the partial explanations of the human behavior that is the subject matter of psychoanalysis; psychology and the gamut of social sciences provide the other. Brain changes are but links in the chain of phenomenological events. It would be an error to eliminate or downplay either. A loss, for example, leads to mourning or depression, which is associated with activation of the amygdala. The activated cerebral location did not "cause" the depression, even if the affect could not have eventuated without it. Psychoanalysis does not belong to neurology, nor is it totally of sociology or history; it belongs to both and is superordinate to all.

One might feel, with the new developments in neuroscience, as if Freud's research a century ago into the synapse between neuron and idea, or nerve conduction and specific affect, has been resumed and advanced in this modern turn. But while one hopes, patience is still in order. From whichever side research is done, the advances remain limited to that side of the duality, without a significant crossing over from one modality to the other. Certainly nothing has been advanced as to what takes place at the synapse between a neuron and an idea, or an impulse and affect, or any aspect of the body and a thought or feeling. Greenacre (1963) said long ago that however much is known about brain functioning, the mystery of creativity remains. This applies as well to the most routine and mundane thought or decision. Freud's negative conclusions in his project have not been advanced to any degree in the molecular way that Freud worked. No visualization of the brain will explain the contents of a phobia, nor will any unconscious fantasy and its accompanying affects be specifically localized in any cerebral nucleus or cell, thereby subjecting it to treatment by a specific organic intervention.

The same applies to the role of the culture as to that of the brain—that is, to the external links in the chain of events as to the internal somatic organs involved. Neither the brain nor the culture creates the neurosis, or brings about conflicts of ideas and affects, or gives form to the compromise formations that are fashioned as solutions. To overlook the role of either leaves the explanation incomplete, but even both together do not make up the entire cycle. The complex human neurotic syndrome cannot arise or take its shape without the complementary functioning of all aspects of its host's brain, body, world, and mind. Developmentally, from birth on, the infant enters life with his soma, his hard drive, which is acted upon and further sculpted by his experiences with people and things.

Another relation between theory and the issue of nonmedical analysis, and the present return, even stampede, back to the brain, has been suggested by Bronstein (2005). Medical practitioners, suffering the competition of the large influx of new members, are turning to neuroscience and pharmacotherapy readily, at the expense of psychotherapeutic approaches, which are diminishing. Seeing a possible cause and effect in this trend, Bronstein writes, "I fear the other issue is the problem with the loss of medical identity to many of our M.D. degree analysts. Ever since the Gaskill amendment, with all its opposition, was passed and the number of analysts who are not medical has increased, there has been a noticeable push towards more biologically based explanations for mental health illnesses and the immense increase in the use of medications both in adult and child treatments and noticeably in psychoanalytic treatments as well."

An observation I would make, however, to this suggestion is the parallel increase in the role of neuroscience among psychologists as well, to which the work in this area of Fonagy, Schore, and others attests. The relations between theory and practical aspects of practice are not to be ignored, but I would point out that such a potential or actual connection is not limited to physicians. Many psychologists also wish and seek prescription privileges, and, like the physicians, coverage for this while they also practice psychological therapy. My experience with the issues of turf and practical self-interest is that this is not limited to one profession but applies to human life. I have stressed the normalcy of narcissism and have written (1974, 1976, 1980) of the ubiquity of C of I (the syndrome of the compromise of integrity) and its application to every aspect of civilized (and uncivilized?) group life.

The relationship of psychoanalysis to the medical profession has been a phasic and changeable one, related to large movements of public opinion as well as to long periods of testing the practical performance of the new profession. Having been situated within the medical fold at its official entrance to this country, shortly after Freud's first and only visit to the United States, in Massachusetts and New York, there was at first a dubious take, with medical schools and the medical profession being slow to assimilate the new implant. Serendipity then played a part when the first, followed by the second, great war presented unusual opportunities through which the military and the public suddenly came to see an unexpected fit. World War II, in particular, amplified this acceptance in a major way when dynamic (i.e., analytic) psychiatry was applied widely and acquired unexpected respect. It is well known that in the aftermath of the war, psychoanalysis spread, took firm root, and became virtually household knowledge. The medical schools followed suit. In the 1950s and 1960s, chairmen of departments of psychiatry in the most prestigious medical schools were mostly psychoanalysts.

Since the 1970s, with the developmental progression I have been describing and documenting, the psychoanalysts are out again, back into the defensive position in which they have mostly resided. The honeymoon with medicine, though lasting rather long, is over. Psychopharmacology and neuroanatomy are back strong. While an effort is in progress to make this phase integrative of both fields, the outcome is uncertain. Continuing balance is needed, and the science of the two, fused and acting together, is awaited.

This history is by way of understanding how the original group decisions in this country came to pass. It does not claim to explain or justify the resistance that endured for the many decades after that, keeping the two large divisions apart, with bitter feelings simmering. The causative factors of the prolonged separation were, as usual, multidetermined. While the delay in effecting an even position was, in its origins at least, in part due to the concrete historical factors I have described, its continuation was sustained by relations between groups with conflicting interests, old and young, new and old. Neurotic group mechanisms played a part, probably no more or less than is seen in all of human history—internecine rivalry that is worse between close ones, the closer the worse, as between older and younger siblings, or even between parents and children. Narcissism and self-interests played as much of a role as in all human relationships. There were more and less rational participants on both sides of all these dualities. And there is enough C of I to go around. Clarity, rationality, and morality have no better record in the psychoanalytic group process than they have had in other social, political, or scientific groups.

The two roots of psychoanalysis, its biological and psychological moorings, existed from the beginning within theory, not particularly clashing with one another. The pioneer theoreticians, from different cultures, each contributed whatever parts of the whole were synchronous with his (there were no females at that stage) history and interest, existing side by side, with agreements and beginning separations, with no relation to previous fields of origin. On the basic, underlying scientific level, Freud himself tried to bridge the two domains that his new discoveries were bringing together, until, as is known, he put the project aside. The two concurrent streams of motivational energy making for neuroses have remained an unsolved dichotomy to this day without being able to be scientifically fused. New attempts have become prominent, but I believe they have a long way to go. A process of integration is necessary here that is yet to come. That would be an epic day.

The contributions of psychoanalysis to the role of the mind are no reflection on the value of organic approaches to mental problems and conflicts, which have their own legitimate and authentic indications. But the introduction of the science of the input of the mind can prevent an overuse of either the mental or somatic alone. In a realistic sense, as one who has been a neurologist first, I am aware and cautious to prevent this pendular swing, to keep a proper balance by now not permitting an overuse again of the role of the organic nervous system in functional mental disease. The swing back to the brain now has a built-in governor. Trainees in the mind alone need to gain this balance, as those steeped primarily in the soma need to acquire the role of the spirit.

AND THE BODY

The same interaction as between mind and brain is true also of the relation of mind to the body in general. Interrelationships between the physical and the mental are among the most complex in human science. A more diffuse interface than that between the mind and the brain are the interactions of the mind and emotions with the whole body. As Freud (1923) said, "The ego is first and foremost a bodily ego" (26). At a meeting of the German Psychoanalytic Association in 1983 on psychosomatic processes, I (2000) said,

> It is difficult to achieve a scientific explanatory balance for the organic and psychological together. Chemical, pharmacologic, endocrinologic, neuroanatomical, electrical and radiologic studies have resulted in a massive

> advance in knowledge of somatic, especially central nervous system functioning. But all of these combined continue to add up to an advance on the physiological side of the border, coming toward the psychological but not into it. Endorphins, which protect against pain, do not answer the riddles of anxiety; nor do anxiolytic agents or antidepressant drugs cast light on the psychological causes, mechanisms or results of anxiety or depression. Even in the field of sleep and dream research, where the border between the psychic and somatic is often the field of investigation, knowledge accrues on each side, not, I am afraid, between the two. Gerard (1959) stated that not every twisted thought leaves a twisted molecule. And Kety (1960) pointed out that there can one day be a chemistry of memory but not of memories. The same applies to dreaming as compared to dreams. Our understanding of the conditions of sleep and the timing of dreams is continuously expanded, but not equally the analytic knowledge of the contents of the dream. The psychological contents of anxiety or depression cannot be gleaned from the chemicals which can exert an influence on the clinical severity of the respective affects. (181–82)

While that statement was made twenty years ago and has never been updated, I feel that it still holds. Dreaming may be increasingly illuminated by an understanding of the underlying neurophysiological processes, but no dream will ever be interpreted by a PET scan. Nor is it likely that the veracity of a recovered memory will one day be confirmed or denied by X-ray evidence.

ADD, NOT REPLACE: RETAIN THE MEDICAL

As brain localization expanded to include affective and wider mental phenomena, including visual proof of the effects of psychotherapy, the new findings of brain representations of psychic processes made more complex the theoretical issue of where the discipline of psychoanalysis fits into the family of science. Was it these findings that made a science out of psychoanalysis? Did psychoanalysis depend on such verification? Was psychoanalysis not a science before and unless organic confirmation was achieved?

Freud pondered over this dilemma during his entire creative life, from his scientific attempt to solve it via the Project (1895) to his concerns as to who should practice psychoanalysis. It was Freud's decision to embark on a career in medicine, and the fact that his new discoveries were thereby born in the process of therapy—of the neurotic symptomatology of the times—that set the discipline quite automatically in the domain of medicine. Freud himself, moreover, strongly motivated to have his brainchild accepted by the scientific establishments and authorities of the time, fought to remain authentic and to be included in the prestigious institutions of his surround. Nevertheless, his struggle is well known. With his bent for higher, abstract philosophical thinking, social conscience, and his deep resonance for the breakthrough implications of his interests and discoveries, simple conclusions did not sit well; complexity and ambiguity were often the outcomes. His defense of Theodore Reik, who became the first psychoanalyst to be challenged legally for a layperson practicing therapy, stated his final opinion. With the new ecology in the American after the lawsuit in 1987, an opposite view away from medicine gathered strength, and "Whose psychoanalysis is it?" (Brooks and Woloch 2000) became a subject of panels as charged as any discussions of competitive theories, and as subjectively attended. To many, a separate and independent category of science was needed, neither solely anatomical-physiologic nor exclusively social. Hartmann (1958) felt that an intermediate realm of science between the physical and social sciences is the home area for the new body of thought. Anna Freud wished for a new university department, a separate channel in the intellectual spectrum.

Again, all parts are necessary for the whole, and a continuum of phenomenology is the actual living event. While neuroscience should not now leave the mind behind, for a retrospective look to be complete, the inclusion of psychoanalysis as a discipline into the social sciences, which was Freud's wish, should also not be followed by an exclusion or minimizing of its root in medicine. This would be an error in the opposite direction, which, in this pendular history, would not be unexpected. While the mind moves out into the wider world of intellect and society, it should not thereby leave the brain or the body behind.

In the long neglect of social vis à-vis physical science, it is what was omitted that was at fault, not what was laboriously built. And again, the rational path is to add, not replace. As the brain and neurological sciences were not sufficient to explain the mind and its contents, the mind does not exist without the brain. The brain, as we all know, is now returning into the limelight, to some extent again with excessive expectations. While the medical-sociological division has vexed the practice of psychoanalysis through most of the century, this dichotomy has not overlapped the theoretical splits. From the beginning, divisiveness in the theory and understanding of the mind had little to do with the medical degree. Freud, Jung, and Hartmann were physicians; Rank, Waelder, and Erikson were not.

It would also be unfortunate if the former exclusion of the social scientist were followed by a denigration or exclusion of the physical or medical one. I would admonish that a swing of the pendulum in the opposite direction should be guarded against, which would be a new exclusivity, now the reactive elimination of the medical and the brain. The present situation, where in some institutes there is one MD in a candidate class, is an ominous sign. The same is true in reverse of medical schools, or departments of psychiatry, without psychoanalysts. In my opinion, the complete psychoanalyst should have roots and expertise in everything human: a person's body and brain; the external societal life in which his brain navigates; and, most microscopically, the mind intermediate between the two, which mediates the interactions between the person—or self, entity, or organism—and the maze of the external world that it interacts with, both affecting it and being nourished and stimulated by it at the same time. The human being, with the unique combined action of both, represents the highest development on the planet. To aim to sit astride the whole, the mental product and the brain from which it derives, is an awesome goal. The complete psychoanalyst is a humanistic scientist, a scientific humanist.

12

THE SCIENCE

LAY ANALYSIS AND THE SCIENCE OF PSYCHOANALYSIS

To focus again on the central question of the course and fate of our theory, has the direction taken and the alternatives that have proliferated borne any relation to this particular division among analysts according to disciplines of origin from which analysts derive? Has the history of separation according to medical versus nonmedical background affected the course of development of the explanatory theory or theories that are at the heart of psychoanalysis today?

Actually, the issue of the prior training or profession of the future analyst does have a bearing on theory, and on the place of psychoanalysis in science, but not on the theoretical dichotomy of unity-pluralism with which it is confused. From the beginning band of pioneers, and continuously since, the problem of eligibility to practice psychoanalysis was related to the question, what is this new psychoanalysis and where does it belong in the family of science?

Straddling the border between the physical and social sciences, the place of the new field posed a question from the beginning. Freud himself was obviously poised between the two, feeling that it belonged to both, or at one time to a species of its own, until finally, in his most important statement in 1926, it was a branch of psychology. First Freud

(1895) tried to bridge the two scientifically by delineating a Project for a Scientific Psychology—it was to be medicine *and* psychology, involving a system of neurons connected to cognition, affects, repression, and primary process, an effort that did not lead to practical or enduring results—which Freud started and then gave up. Some today are considering whether this early effort can relate to present-day developments in neuroscience. Here was an attempt at the very start to blend, or to find the connecting links, the psychobiological synapses, between the two, the nervous system and the psyche.

Freud puzzled over this major question from the beginning of his investigations and insights. His early intellectual interests were manifold, spanning across disciplines and serving as the complex background of this permanently vexing problem. His influences from the University of Vienna and thereafter spanned from the likes of Brentano to Meynert to Charcot, from philosophy to neurological science. Freud's decision to study medicine, however ambivalently come to, was crucial for him, and later for many of his followers, to position the new discipline within the biological sciences, and as such within natural science. But this did not exclude his perplexity as to the physical versus the social sciences. From the beginning, the mental might be in a class of its own. The path, the line, the leap between the brain and the idea, or the reverse direction, from the thought to the soma, was never demonstrable; it was always deduced. Freud, however, remained forever in conflict over this elusive synapse. His attempt via the project to establish the position of the mental within the somatic, the idea and affect inside the brain, psychoanalysis into neurology, did not succeed and was suspended not abandoned; Freud still entertained future hopes for somatic and perhaps even chemical solutions to mental conflicts.

But after putting aside this intense focused attempt, Freud's entire subsequent career, as he defined and structuralized the mental world, saw Freud and his growing supporters exploring the entire inner and outer surrounds of the individual, from genetic and microdynamic internal factors to the widest social, historical, and environmental inputs. Contiguous disciplines were eagerly examined and their contributions absorbed, including art, literature, history, anthropology, mythology, paleontology, and every other pursuit of intellectual man.

Every step of the way brought contradictory appraisals. Bergmann (2004), writing on "dissidence and controversy," states that "Freud, wanting to make psychoanalysis a part of natural science, did not give due consideration to the impact of culture" (96), and that, by overemphasizing the clinical at the expense of the cultural, Freud failed to make psychoanalysis a general psychology. Schneider and Desmond (1994) stated the opposite. It was the medical focus brought about by the politics of exclusion, they wrote, that favored the clinical over the cultural and blocked a general psychology, contrary to Freud's view. Freud is credited, and debited, with opposite views. Bergmann (2000) also spells out the end of the Hartmann era, the same Hartmann who added the adaptive point of view, making psychoanalysis a definitive, general theory of behavior, which Bergmann wishes for.

The fact is that the clinical, practice and theory, and a general psychology feed each other, as Waelder (1962) pointed out about clinical and abstract theory. Clinical findings lead to abstract understanding, and abstract theory guides the clinical process. The same applies to a clinical and a general theory. Each contributes to the construction of the other.

WHOSE PSYCHOANALYSIS IS IT?

The question of where the newfound body of knowledge was to be planted existed, in an unspoken form, immediately as the new discoveries were made. The "lay analysis" label, an uncomfortable one that required a redefinition, which Freud provided in 1926, was not imposed but arose from a number of serendipitous circumstances and developments that brought the issue into full view. Alternate directions evolved as soon as the field was born and started to progress. Freud was a physician; after the widest education and scope of interests, he had become a medical student, then a physician. He studied and began to contribute to neurology, neuropathology, neuroanatomy, and biological science. He had spawned off of Charcot, the iconic French neurologist. But he was zeroing in on the mind, on the wispy and intangible, and the staid medical establishment was looking askance. He was grazing on soil that had always been the hunting ground of mystics, adventurers, eccentrics, the daring, and the curious. The discipline constructed upon this wild terrain was fashioned by a man of medicine, but with a wide, cultured past and present. The famous Egyptian collection on his desk tells that story.

Freud himself was ambivalent about medicine and the medical establishment. But his identity, and the subject of his interest, led to the brain and the mind. The outcome, a new field of investigation and explanation, led to a question: where does this new profession belong in the family of science?

That the origins of the new science came via therapy and not initially by an exploration of any of man's external, creative products was not accidental but necessary. The fact that the first experiences with psychoanalysis were in the area of therapy, not social or artistic or aesthetic or cultural issues, and that Freud approached the new clinical terrain as a neurologist, planted the field originally in the realm of medicine. The later American position that located the new discipline in the medical field, bitterly resented by so many, did not come about in a vacuum, but as a sequel connected to its origin and early development. Art, literature, and history came later. It had to be in this sequence, for method and for motivation. It could not have been the reverse; one could not have observed the data from the opposite direction. But later extensions of the theory and a growing applied body of knowledge continued to bring to the fore the same question of the locus of the field in its expertise, and related to this, the qualifications of its practitioners.

The dichotomy "clinical versus applied" appeared at once as the early rush of discoveries was being made. Clinical observations at first made possible clinical applications. The latter multiplied into other fields exponentially as time passed. With both poles actively operative—the clinical as source, the applied as result—the question was, at the outset, where does psychoanalysis fit into the family of science? With later expansion, it became, whose psychoanalysis is it? And as the field continued to widen, the question emerged, what remains the relation of the clinical to all future developments?

THE COUCH AND THE WORLD

The answer to all of these related queries is that the clinical is the core and the applications the wide periphery, and both take place in every analysis, even if the application is limited to the treatment of the patient. Applied analysis spreads from an individual treatment to almost every pursuit of man, the element in common being human motivation. While the likelihood of the full psychoanalytic process ever becoming a mass activity is obviously unrealistic, analytically oriented psychotherapy in a myriad of forms has invaded the intellectual world, and, as I (2001) have pointed out, this will be the most ubiquitous legacy of psychoanalytic knowledge. Every variant of therapy makes use of a greater or lesser number of its insights and methods.

For creating the atmosphere to uncover and traverse defenses, the proper motivational incentives are required. Anxiety in general serves this function clinically. The patient's ego-alien affects are enlisted to overcome resistances. The clinical situation, in my opinion, is the original research, at the source of the depth of human psychology—the arena for uncovering defenses and resistances and the repressed contents that are being obscured. That this remains necessary as the database for the contents of the unconscious from which additions and modifications can be discovered is not disputable. The body of knowledge of the science of psychoanalysis could not have derived from the reverse direction, from applied analysis first. Leads do emanate from any direction, from works of art, literature, manuscripts, scrolls, artifacts, and excavations, but confirmation from free associations of living beings, who can confirm or deny, is scientifically central.

Increasing application brings with it more perplexing or global questions. With the new science spreading its applicability to virtually all activities of man, given that the mind is in all cases the agent of their execution, both before and after the official admission of nonmedical practitioners on a large scale, but more so afterward, the question was posed, "Whose Freud?" as in the panel on that subject held at Yale. Dealing with the status of psychoanalysis in contemporary culture, the question explored was whether there has been a wholesale displacement of psychoanalysis from its central area of relevance in the clinical situation to academia.

It would indeed be regrettable if the clinical center of psychoanalysis and any aspect of applied analysis were considered mutually exclusive, or if displacement to any other area is what is thought to have taken place. In my assessment of the future of psychoanalysis, the clinical survives, as well as its applications to every aspect of culture, universities included. In elaborating on this, I have foretold that analytic psychotherapy will be the largest segment of the application of the treatment situation, although psychoanalysis itself will always endure as the source of the ongoing expansion and discoveries at the psychic depth—as well as retaining its permanent role in the training of analysts.

The question, to whom does psychoanalysis belong? has more theoretical relevance than might be apparent. Thinking about where psychoanalysis fits—whether into the family of science or among the social disciplines—has always been a provocative intellectual game. Freud discovered, or invented, the science of the mind. But whether psychoanalysis is a science, an art, or a craft (Gray 2000) became a debatable subject. It is all of these. Its history and goals were, from the beginning, modeled after the tenets of science, observation, deduction, theory formation, validation, and, hopefully, although difficulties were at once predictable, replicability and falsifiability. And if it is a science, is it a natural science or not? I (2002) agreed with Brenner (1999), who answers that question in the affirmative. Nature makes no exceptions. The mind is derivative of the brain and ceases to exist when the brain dies. Yet the mind is more than the brain, although it cannot exist without it. After separating psychoanalysis from existential philosophy and claiming the new discipline for science, Hartmann concluded that the new discipline belonged not to the physical but to the social sciences, which have their own methodologies, criteria, and means of validation. Freud envisioned the field he discovered as an overall science of man. The mind nurtures, and is nurtured by, humanity; it grows into and is fed by its social surround. This does not exclude mental science from the natural science. Natural science must include human science. Nature includes human nature.

All of these apparent polarities—between natural and behavioral science, for example, and between science and art (or craft)—as with most of the dualities we have confronted, are better seen as varying degrees of combination. The intellectual issue posed by the broad new array of social and behavioral scientists entering the field does not devolve into lay *or* medical but affects each equally. To any analyst, from whatever path, the theory and science of psychoanalysis encompasses brain and behavior, body and mind, person and society, the realms of the physician and of the psychologist/mentalist both.

13

THE BREAKUP OF TECHNIQUE

FROM THE 1990s: CHANGING PATTERNS OF THE THEORY OF TECHNIQUE

To return from this digression—the issue of where psychoanalysis fits into science, which came about because of the confluence of the American Psychoanalytic Association with ego psychology; a discussion of the negative aura against the American on that account, which led to the hostility toward the American also over the question of lay analysis; a plea about the necessity to keep these two issues separate and to judge the American theoretical position on its own; and then the relation of the lay analysis issue itself to the science of psychoanalysis—now, after these relevant diversions, we go back to our chronological account of the development and undulations of psychoanalytic theory.

As the ambience of abstract pluralism settled in, the last two decades have seen another type of divisiveness appear as smaller innovations proliferated more freely than before, affecting mainly the theories of technique, although behind these, the wider theories upon which they stand as well. The result has been to split practitioners as well as theoreticians into an increasing number of factions. I can say briefly about this next period that significant numbers from time to time gathered behind leaders who advocated or emphasized one specific aspect of technique, or one segment of the theory of technique, and, true to the built-in fallacy of pars pro toto, would elevate that part to a whole. If the leader did not quite do this, the followers did. In this category, I would mention, as a sampling, enactment, self-disclosure, two-person psychology, intersubjectivity, the social-constructivist position, and countertransference on a par with transference as the method of treatment. At a somewhat more abstract rather than clinical-technical level is attachment theory, and the latest within it, mentalization.

Coming in rapid succession, most of these modernly advocated concepts, automatically considered "liberal" in contrast to preexisting "conservative" positions, aimed to loosen up what was considered a previous rigid position on the part of the analyst, or an asymmetrical relationship between the two participants, in the service of a more democratic or even relationship between patient and analyst. Although to do justice to any one of these would require a more in-depth description, I will of necessity take these up briefly, in summary form, and mainly refer to some characteristics in common of these various quick developments.

SELF-DISCLOSURE

One such movement was self-disclosure. The course of events was typical for all. In this case, Renik (1993), the main spokesman for this chosen new emphasis, writes on the "irreducible subjectivity" in the analyst, with which all analysts can agree, and which is part of the traditional analyzing instrument. He then goes on, however, to recommend and demonstrate his own preferred technical means of communicating to the patient what goes on in his own mind to an extent that is generally more than has been the accustomed practice. To issues that arise, he shares memories of his own affective life and historical development, describing that these "work" in producing therapeutic benefit. More than this, he (1996) points out the "perils of neutrality," that neutrality is counterproductive, and that if indeed it can be achieved, "[neutrality] removes the analyst from the field. In order for a dialectical learning process to unfold, the analyst's active, personally motivated participation is required" (507). While some of Renik's clinical examples go much further than many older analysts would have considered necessary or desirable, others are in a gray area with which all can agree, and I do not feel in general that they did any violence or harm to the analytic situation.

What followed, however, in the years that this view elicited a group excitement typical for this genre of innovations, was an atmosphere in which personal revelation became almost the required mode, stressed by conforming faculty and adopted by compliant candidates. During this period, it was routine for students in supervision to report, as one did to me, "The patient said she had received a gift of a sporting new convertible, and I told her I felt envious," or to share fantasies or verbalize a feeling of attraction, often to the confusion or anxiety of the patient, if not approaching a slippery slope of untoward iatrogenic collusion. Renik (1997) himself comes back to a view that can be generally shared, that disclosure takes place to the extent that it is to the interest of the patient, not the analyst. But the influence of the stretched innovation has gone further than he has, and for a while constituted a new "school." It also, during its heyday, influenced many psychotherapists who use analytic theory and emulate analysts.

ENACTMENT

The same sequence and experience involves the subject of enactment, which for a few years became a buzzword at the advance edge of "modern" technique. Introduced first on solid analytic ground, pointing to behavioral rather than verbal responses on the part of the analyst useful in conveying interpretations, increasing attention is paid to actions in analysis on the parts of both patient and analyst. In time, however, these become hypertrophied and over-used, accompanied by a minimalization of the value of the usual verbal exchanges. Dissatisfied with the slow course of traditional treatment, many analysts come to feel that words lead to intellectuality and impasses, and that the answer is not talk but action. Suddenly analysis becomes more active. The central mechanism of thought as experimental action is by-passed. Action superseding thought becomes the analyst's new therapeutic tool; we learn what we think by what we do.

What at first is a helpful emphasis runs a biphasic course. While careful analysis of all observable data, actions as well as words, yields a richer understanding, a new passion, to analyze by doing, "enacting" (acting outward), becomes a false distraction, a new form of acting-out or acting-in. Again, lessons and experiences from the past are obliterated or minimized. It is not as if actions have not always been an integral part of the analytic process. Words have never served alone. Analysis has always recognized nonverbal communications. Posture, gestures, vocal tones, affective signals have always been within the analyst's purview; and on the analyst's side, such actions are an integral accompaniment of routine interpretations. In "very disturbed" analytic situations, more complex trial actions have indeed also been used, although hardly without trial thought. But these are usually the exceptions; the analytic means of communication are basically by language, which still holds.

It is important to keep in mind the line of differentiation between acting-out, an unconscious intrapsychic phenomenon, and enactment as a technical mode of analytic communication. At an IPA panel in Copenhagen in 1967, I (1968) pointed out, along with Anna Freud (1968) and Vanggaard (1968), that acting-out during analysis, whether within or external to the analytic situation, is on the same plane as a symptom, and as such is to be analyzed, without pejorative implications. Enactments, on the other hand, as communication within the technical armamentarium of the analyst, is a different aspect of analytic action. After a period of excitement, this new emphasis reaches faddish proportions, and is then less heard from.

INTERSUBJECTIVITY

Many other separate segments of the analytic encounter have been chosen for special emphasis, mostly single issues made into major aspects of theory or technique and offered as alternatives to the existing sweep of total Freudian theory. Enactment and self-disclosure were followed, or accompanied, by intersubjectivity, which has become an overall quality stressed in most modern or contemporary approaches. In this mode, as in the most popular relational school at its center, psychoanalysis is emphasized as a two-person psychology, or a social-constructivist relationship, highlighting the equality of patient and analyst, as though the assumption of the analyst and patient roles in treatment assumes the same asymmetric position in life. Countertransference is placed on a par with transference, and with some analysts is considered the means of treatment. The thought behind this equal pairing seems to be that to concentrate on transference alone is one sided and unfair to the patient; the analyst must match him or her. This is akin to an analyst who said at a panel, "I don't like resistances," feeling that to point out a resistance or defense is an insult or put-down of the patient.

The psychoanalytic method, supported by its theory, has always been intersubjective and two person, along with its being asymmetric in the conduct of an analysis. Affects and subjectivity are in the analyst as well as the patient, in the analyzing instrument and in the subjects of the analysis. But the goals of each and the uses of each in the pair working together are sharply different. To confuse the asymmetric roles of patient and analyst with the roles of the two in life disregards the inputs of psychoanalytic theory and its theory of technique.

The traditional approach, regarded as a one-person, positivistic psychology, is pictured in its stark form as interpretation and insight provided by an uninvolved (and uncaring) analyst, who is a screen for transference, who comes to know the truth of the patient's past, and who delivers it to the thankful patient. This is of course rightly comic and is the stuff of cartoons and caricature. If it ever existed, it is now invisible. Upon a nucleus of this attitude that might have been clumsily true, much has been added or has even accompanied it in the past. From Freud on, traditional analysts combined their analytic search with a deep devotion to the patient's welfare and security. Humanness and empathy need always to be fused with the objective attitude necessary to pursue the analytic goal; indeed, the latter cannot really be brought about without at least the necessary amount of the former. But while analysis was always between two persons, there are also differences. Analysis is not undertaken to treat two neuroses. The subjectivity of the analyst is primarily in the service of his analyzing instrument, however much his separate and idiosyncratic affects play a part as well. The subjectivity on the part of the analyst, which is always there, is a factor that works for or against the analysis and needs always to be taken into account, but his objectivity is a sine qua non of his functioning as an analyst.

These various technical innovations merge into the subject prominent in the 1950s, where the emphasis was to define and preserve the line between psychoanalysis and its derivative psychotherapies (Gill 1954; Rangell 1954a; Stone 1954). In a follow-up of this subject twenty-five years later (Gill 1979; Rangell 1981b; Stone 1979), the line was seen to be a band; more of each was included in the other. Today, with further developments in the analytic method and the use of parameters, the theoretical issue still exists, now to define this still-wider band. Much of relational and enactment treatment merges into what was analytic dynamic psychotherapy, without any pejorative meaning; the treatment is fitted to the patient. The amount of retention of analytic theory and practice determines how much of each obtains. However much the two overlap, I still feel today, as I wrote in 1954, that, while there is a wide field of overlap between the two contiguous treatments, there is still a separation between the two techniques. From my paper on this subject of 1954, "Day is different from night, though there is dusk; and black from white, though there is gray (with no implications as to one being right or wrong, better or worse)" (737).

While psychoanalysis has taught us with great force that conflicts coexist, this has not been the same with contradictions, which are mutually exclusive. A patient cannot trace his anxiety or other unease to unresolved conflict with one analyst and to inherited or constitutional defect with another and emerge with the same mind-set or restitutional powers, or with the same conviction of his own role in the past or in requirements for his future. Or, if he can, in spite of what is told him, it is his doing, not a claim for the validity of the science; the patient puts things together his own way. A discipline replete with contradictions at its intellectual base can hardly present itself as a science to guide suffering human beings to where they wish to go.

THE RATIONAL EGO

I have lived and worked with general satisfaction under Fenichel's dictum "The subject matter, not the method, of psychoanalysis is irrational" (1941, 13; also in 1945, 4). My life applying the theory of psychoanalysis to the varied experiences of a psychoanalytic clinician has given me no reason to abandon this guideline. I have found the multipronged theory of psychoanalysis applicable across the board, ready to be applied to the infinite situations we are privileged to confront in our daily work. Irrationalities do not worry or deflect us; they are what we seek and welcome, as subjects of our study.

Affects, however, that are of use within our analyzing instrument are used, to paraphrase Ernst Kris (1936), in the service of the analyzing ego. Any intrusion into the instrument beyond this function should neither surprise us nor be embraced. Primary process thinking is as pervasive and determining as secondary logic in the very atmosphere in which we live. There is no reason to be thrown off course when this occurs in the analyst during the course of his work. Flaws and fallacies have been visible as subjects in the history of our science and in our body politic as routinely as in the subject matter we aim to treat. But our corrective insights should operate to keep the methods and goals on course.

Quite often, these irrational incursions into the analytic instrument itself, and through that into the analytic process, which need to be recognized and corrected, are instead welcomed and considered a source for self-congratulations. This is often the case in the special technical deviations above or, more routinely, with a disturbed or disturbing patient, or in a difficult clinical impasse with any patient, where an abandonment of a rational process can be premature and itself rationalized. It is as though laxity and lapses, which may be unavoidable, are regarded instead as flexibility, which is desirable. As the antidote to this, to quote Fenichel (1941) again, "treatment is through the rational ego"; the aim is to explain the irrational by the rational; technique "must be arranged according to rational criteria" (13). This is not to say that the rational next step may not mean changing the method and the goals. That is daily the case in a clinical life. The variations in challenging clinical phenomena in a general psychoanalytic practice are as infinite as people are.

Changes go on continuously; the questions are which and how much. Consider as an example the anonymity of the analyst. Early analysts carried anonymity to an extreme, for reasons guided by initial theory, but it turns out that they misjudged its importance as well as its practicality. Certainly change has come about, and the analytic attitude with regard to the openness of the analyst underwent much transformation about the analyst revealing aspects of himself. The initial blank facade, which evoked much valuable material and knowledge but turned many people off, evolved into a more rational, flexible practice not only by modern deconstruction but by gradual evolution. The same change by incremental evolution has taken place about the natural and overt participation of the analyst in other aspects of the analytic process. Yet many claims for new theories or even alternative systems have been made on the basis of significant changes in these aspects of the analytic situation. One might say that it was not novelty but excess that usually led to dissident movements. An examination of these trends, I have proposed in this study, suggests that such claims have often gone on to opposite extremes that distorted the development of the science and contributed to its being treated with scorn.

14

THE SOLUTION: TOTAL COMPOSITE PSYCHOANALYTIC THEORY

AN ALTERNATIVE TO ALTERNATIVE THEORIES

There is in fact an alternative to alternative theories, and it has maintained its identity throughout this era of undulating changes. In the ongoing debate over "one theory," I (1988, 1997, 1998, 2004) favor one total, composite psychoanalytic theory, unified and cumulative: total because it contains all nonexpendable elements, composite because it is a blend of the old and all valid new concepts and discoveries, and psychoanalytic as fulfilling the criteria for what is psychoanalysis. Throughout the various phases of changing theories during the last thirty years, I have favored one integrated unitary theory, containing all new advances that are generally considered valid, while retaining all previous discoveries that are not expendable and have endured. My (1955a, 1968) unitary theory of anxiety is an earlier example of such integration, composed of a fusion of both of Freud's theories of anxiety.

At numerous phases of the development of theory, I have shown that a proposed alternative theory has been based upon a retention and expansion of an element of existing theory, accompanied by an unspoken diminution of other elements that empirically still continue to apply. Alongside such changes that have turned out to be divisive, a mainstream theory has grown from its inception to the present, with periodic, cumulative increments that in my opinion have been insufficiently recognized or articulated. I have identified two previous periods when such increments were prominent: the first after the original rush of discoveries, plus the additions stressed in early interpersonal and cultural theories, and the second in the 1950s following World War II, with the elaboration of the ego. My present description, merging the many separate theoretical and technical spurts since the 1970s, is a third fertile period of the developing composite theory.

By such a process of consolidation, aiming to achieve a livable togetherness of all valid contributed parts, the total theory comes to contain, in a manner accommodating all of its components, a coherent unity. Every contributor can recognize and take credit for his unique discovery or emphasis—Kohut for the self, Renik for the analyst's more uninhibited participation, Schwaber for the liberated functioning of empathic affect by the analyst, Chused for the more spontaneous use of action and the body. Each illuminated an area that stood the whole well. But all can act without the expulsion of the drives, or of any of the enduring parts, or of analytic objectivity and the subordination of all aspects of the process to understanding the unconscious levels of the patient's functioning.

WHAT IS INCLUDED?

What is included in total composite theory? Every viable contribution made by alternative theories is to be added to all aspects of preceding theory that remain enduring. Looking at many dichotomies, total theory includes drives and objects, the Oedipal and the pre-Oedipal, constitutional givens and environmental inputs, the past and the present, the transference neurosis and the infantile neurosis, conflict and deficit, the cognitive and affective, the self and the ego, the intrapsychic and the interpersonal, the internal and external worlds, nature and nurture, and fantasies of and actual traumata. Historical truth and narrative truths all have their place. The entire human developmental life cycle is included, spanning infancy, childhood, latency, puberty, adolescence, adulthood, maturity, and geriatrics. Each phase leaves its imprint, from the prenatal genetics, to the gestation period, to the birth process, and to all that follows in the outer world.

I include unambivalently all five of Freud's metapsychological points of view, plus the one addition of Rapaport and Gill's (1959) adaptive view. I find all of them useful and each contributory. Though popular development has come to favor eliminating two, the economic and the topographic, I prefer to retain both of these, as well as adding the new adaptive view stemming from Hartmann's adaptive functions of the ego and Rapaport's ego autonomy. I decide this not out of nostalgia or loyalty, but after putting these points of view to the test of observational validity and technical relevancy. Two allies in this inclusiveness are Anna Freud (in Sandler and A. Freud 1985) and, more modernly, Schmidt-Hellerau (2001). I do not feel that the structural eliminated the topographic view, nor do I agree with the discarding of the economic because of its inability to fulfill the criteria and methodology of physical science. Nor am I concerned that there is overlap, and sometimes no clear lines, between some of these methods of approach, as there are between many other psychological concepts. There are gray areas between the psychic structures, as between ego and superego, and the preconscious connects the conscious and unconscious. There is an ever-widening gray area between psychoanalysis and analytic psychotherapy, without rendering either of them unacceptable. Similarities and differences connect and separate them. As follows from Freud's concepts of overdetermination and the complementary series, explanations and contributions converge from many directions into the final total scheme of an all-embracing understanding.

The new is to be added to what exists and remains viable. Attachment and its accompanying issues are a recent example of a phase or process that is presented as separate but is an intrinsic part of composite theory, as is separation as well. Consider Freud's oral phase and Mahler's separation-individuation stage. These fit snugly and are contained in the elaborations of these by Bowlby, Fonagy, and Tavistock and Hampstead. Modern studies of infancy before the separation process, such as by Stern, cumulate to the earlier works of Spitz, Benjamin, Escalona, Greenacre, and others. Recent studies on mentalization by Fonagy, Target, et al. (2002), who expand the connections of this mental achievement to affect regulation and the development of a self, advance the details of early mental development, all of which are part of total, long-developing Freudian theory.

Attachment and separation, conflictual and adaptive, exist in development and cannot be limited to one system of theory. They have a firm home in the Freudian edifice, in pre-Oedipal life, in the separation-individuation phase, and in the Oedipal experience. Problems of attachment, normal and pathological, have been attended in depth continuously, from Freud to Ferenczi, to Mahler's studies, and to my own work (1955b) on the "quest for ground" in human motivation.

The theory of technique that accompanies composite theory also contains all dichotomies, such as neutrality and empathy, the objective and subjective, reconstruction and the here and now, insight and a new relationship, intersubjectivity and an equidistant analytic position, a nonjudgmental stance and judging where necessary, and passive and active roles of both participants.

In thinking about what is included, I wish to make a special note of the subject of narcissism, which has always been unclear and divisive and has led to separate treatments. After decades of frequent and varied use of this term, the very concept of narcissism has, in my opinion, been one of the most misused, misunderstood, and diversionary subjects in the psychoanalytic enterprise. I believe that the confusion and enigmatic position of this charged word began with Freud as he struggled between his brief first division of instincts as between libidinal and self-preservative ones and his subsequent duality of libidinal and aggressive instincts, followed later by a separate system ego, part of the structural view. From these elements, Freud, as well as his later collaborators and colleagues, emerged with several confusing and ambiguous formulations about the role of self and object love, from which future clinicians and theoreticians came to equate narcissism with "the more disturbed," and subsequently Kohut and self psychologists described a separate line of development entirely for narcissistic motivations.

In my view, a much simpler view of narcissism holds. Whether in the sense of Hartmann's (1958) pithy definition of "the ego's love of the self," an internal appraisal combining the structural and the holistic view, or in its meaning of love of the self as contrasted to love of others, which is more a focus on its external significance, narcissism, in all its ramifications, is as seamless a part of the total human psychological experience as anxiety. An absence of narcissism can be as pathological as an excess. An increase in the trait of narcissism is of the same import and similar universal frequency as the presence of an anxiety state. Neither narcissism nor anxiety in itself bespeaks a malignant condition, nor does either arise from a separate line of development.

In no way does narcissism require or lead to a separate theoretical entity differentiated from the main frame. In its normal or pathological configurations, variations in narcissism fit into and are to be explained by the same total theoretical tree of drives, defenses, affects, compromise formations, symptom formation, and character traits.

Many other central explanatory concepts or preferred modes of technical approaches, a multiplicity of them, currently included in the wide variety of alternative theories, belong naturally and easily within the total theory. While verbal communication is the routine method, action, affects, and posture, all aspects of enactment, also fit without conflict into the traditional, total armamentarium in numerous, almost everyday variations during routine analytic hours. Neither enactment nor any of the other special techniques needs or qualifies for a special place. I also claim the right to retain memory, desire, and understanding, which, for many, separates Bion from others, within my total theoretical frame, while still being able to say that I am also open to new ideas. Theory guides; it is not imposed. The same goes for necessary self-disclosures, as for every parameter or flexible deviation from the center. All remain parts of standard technique, applied where helpful.

WHAT IS NOT INCLUDED?

What is not included in total theory are idiosyncratic constructions that have served to separate split-off advocacy groups that are either not new or not a significant addition. The self-object, for example, is already in main theory under different guises. Infancy of Kleinian theory is included, but not the concrete fantasies attributed by Kleinians to that early age. A two-person psychology is not part of composite theory in a symmetrical form. Tragic man can be included, but not without guilty man, nor empathy at the expense of neutrality, nor attachment without also the separation-individuation process.

Not one of these concepts is without merit. Any or all of them can elicit valid psychoanalytic interest and may be utilized in many, even average, clinical situations. But each of them can be recognized as existing within the enduring "mainstream" theory, usually under different names or guises and in a wider context. They are, as a group, all part of a larger, all-inclusive theoretical orientation, and as such they are dependent on fusion with and support by contiguous or wider or superordinate embracing concepts.

Thus, for example, the self-object is not an idea that can characterize an entire system or justify a delineation of a separate overarching total theory. Mahler's theoretical additions about the separation-individuation phase have ample room for inclusion of the presenting phenomena that analysts of the self psychology school observe and emphasize when they employ this term (Kohut, moreover, spoke disparagingly of Mahler and denied any resemblance or closeness to her theories). There is no separate self-object, either in the transference, where it is so much stressed in the technical aspects of self psychology theory, or in the phenomenology of life observations. Concretization of the term into a structure residing in the unconscious and guiding behavior is neither necessary nor realistic. Dependency between self and object, or failure of self-differentiation, or self and object representations within the ego, are already-existing related concepts within the larger frame. I (1955b) wrote of "the quest for ground" in human motivation, expanding the motive to fuse with the environment to reach beyond objects, to include a firm connection to the external physical world, to the very ground we stand on. Threats or disturbances to the innate biopsychological need to feel the ground under our feet, and to sense when this is threatened or unstable, result in such common human disequilibria as seasickness, various forms of dizziness, or throwing up in an airplane in, or at times without, turbulence. The big, total theory has limitless applications and can explain whatever we observe.

New theories are necessary when explanations are not forthcoming from existing theory and when additions would add to the understanding of observed phenomena.

WHO DECIDES?

"Who is to decide what gets included?" I am asked on numerous occasions. Is this question any different at any other phase of theory building, or with any other state of our theoretical enterprise? Was it different at the beginning, with the nascent nuclei of differing opinions of the early pioneers? Or with each stage of development of the main theory? Or with the putting forth of any alternative theory? Or with the announcement of the equality of all theories? Or now, with rapprochement of divergent theories? Who decides what is right, or rational, or acceptable or unacceptable with respect to any other aspect of the common theoretical quest? The answer is the same in all: the collective consensus for the generally held theoretical system, each analyst for his individual preferences.

In a recent discussion following my presentation of this group of ideas, Martin Bergmann asked me publicly, "Who is to decide what is to be included and what is left out?" In another context, in a symposium on dissidence in psychoanalysis, he expressed his concern about my composite theory as follows: "His [my] only difficulty would be that not everyone will be persuaded to accept his vision of what is included and what is to be left out of his total composite psychoanalytic theory" (Bergmann 2004, 263). No, that is not the case. As I replied to Bergmann directly, each analyst decides for himself; for the field as a whole, a reasonable consensus is the criterion.

Innumerable concepts, large or small, dot the theoretical landscape for each individual to pass his own judgment. Such modern concepts as "the analytic third," or a focus on the space between objects, including the "analytic space," are there for each analyst to use or not at his discretion and preference. The same applies to many other metaphors, which are thought of by some as imaginative and contributory, while others may feel them to often be overdone in a spirit of zealousness and exuberance.

No theory is a straitjacket. An analyst fashions his tool to his own use and style—and to the needs of each patient. The Oedipus has qualified to be in the trunk of the theoretical tree, presumably by an overwhelming consensus. Projective identification, or the depressive or paranoid position, or the role of the first few months of life, are up to each individual analyst to decide, based on his accumulated experience, and to ponder according to what each patient, or each hour, brings.

Bergmann (2004), who has addressed the problem of dissidence with scholarship and fervor, surveys the issues involved in a book with a group of contributors and aims to come to as close a consensus as one can. Regarding my unified theory, he writes, "It is the denial of the ferocity of the emotions involved in the controversies that ultimately leads me to believe that Rangell's solution is utopian" (263). Bergmann's doubts are shared by many, even authors who basically approve of a single Freudian theory. Richards, for example, expresses the same concerns. "Although it certainly cannot be accused of glossing over genuine theoretical differences, Rangell's approach carries with it the danger of foreclosing consideration of potentially revolutionary departures that question fundamental aspects of the system, or even the system itself. However skeptical we may be about currently available alternative models, we put our scientific principles at risk if we decide in advance that we cannot accept any future paradigm shift in psychoanalysis" (Richards 1999, 18). Richards continues,

> Rangell's total composite theory is in part a personal response to the exigencies of his particular psychoanalytic situation. But however congenial this approach to pluralism may be to many analysts, it is likely to be perceived as dismissive by those outside the international Freudian mainstream. They may view its essentialism as undercutting their prerogative to develop and defend new models, which of course they will do in any case. Much as I admire Rangell's forthright defense of classical principles, *which I regard as closest to my own* [italics mine], we must be wary of abandoning serious dialogue with those beyond our immediate psychoanalytic ken. What is political expedience for us may be political anathema to them. (19)

I agree with these precautions. Along with others who feel that one comprehensive Freudian theory covers the field of observations and experience, I am open to any change, partial or major, but not without applying to it the criteria of the scientific method. While in practice an analyst should approach each hour open to any idea that presents itself, new as well as old, in fact looking always for corrections or additions to theory as it exists now this does not mean to accept every slogan that is peremptorily advocated. I, for example, wish to retain the active use of memory, desire, and understanding, notwithstanding that its opposite, the recommendation to eschew these conventional considerations, has become a catchy phrase as group adherents of Bion are apt to carry it. The "ferocity" of emotions aroused in defense of such phrases, or the "anathema" experienced against analysts who retain traditional and commonsense approaches, needs to be understood, not necessarily catered to. I am open to be shown to which "paradigm switch" this view does an injustice, or which innovative ideas I have been too casual about accepting.

WHY DOES A UNITARY THEORY REMAIN ELUSIVE?

A question I have asked is, why is a unitary theory so elusive? Individual analysts almost always express their view that a unified composite theory would be desirable and welcome. Yet they are quite united in expressing a belief that this is not yet here or is not yet ready to be—to the extent that it makes me wonder, as an analyst, whether they really wish it to be. What explanation can there be for this hesitation to pursue what they believe to be best, and their sensitivity to the offense that would be experienced by others? I suggest a pervasive affective condition: is not the value of diversity, democracy, and differences much more ingrained in this country in this historical era than the deep affective response to unity, which connotes sameness, commonness, and oneness, and at the same time autocracy, authority, and hegemony—that is, communism and fascism rolled into one?

Rugged individualism, the mantra of our democracy, with good reason, is intrinsic to our public persona, our collective identity. Should this societal development and achievement, which is understandable, desirable, and supported in our culture, be the criterion applied to science? Is every theory, like every person, different and equal?

In fact, the increased diversity of paths to training makes it even more important to achieve intellectual unity. Freud, as Darwin, unified diversity. Both are equally resisted, and they both need and are engaged in self-protection. People resist being like everyone else as much as they dread being separated. To be separated and to remain united exert equal pulls. Psychoanalysis becomes a hostile target on both accounts. Its understanding declares people more the same than they wish, and it urges them to separate to achieve autonomy more than they care to. The human species is one, not multiple, separate from its closest primates, although connected.

Why does it seem insurmountable to come to a consensus on the few dozen basic concepts involved?

In our field, is it, as I (1982) have written, the weight and ubiquity of transferences to theory that are at the base of such intramural splintering? These would be at two levels, one the displacement of affects felt toward training analysts onto their theories, and the other the array of defenses, distortions, and compromise outcomes that pervade group life transferred to the theories held by the members of the group. It is both of these, I suggest, plus more. Another mechanism is the prevalence of identification with the products of one's mind ("I am what I think"), which then needs to be protected as one preserves the self. An analyst becomes "a self psychologist," "a classicist," or "a Kleinian," not one who simply thinks that way. When I was a young analyst, we learned about "identification with one's anal products"; here it is identification with one's theory. Is it the narcissism of small, or even large, differences to differentiate one from another, both as an individual and as a small group that is one's own? A group too large cannot achieve synchrony of thought or identification, hence the ethnic minorities within a nation. To espouse one understanding in our field is today not politically correct; at bottom is a common belief that one cannot achieve consensus or unity in the large mass group that we have become.

In 1954, I (1954b) gave a paper to the American that I never published, on "a tertiary gain of symptoms," in which I added to the primary and well-known secondary gains of symptoms another motive that worked toward rendering the symptomatic state persistent and at times static. A patient with a headache that she had had for the better part of her life could not give up her symptom after many years of analysis, by which time we both felt we had analyzed it quite thoroughly. The reason, I ventured, was that she now had absorbed the headache into her "ego identity," a concept popular at that time—later, we would say the symptom had become part of her self-representation. She *was* "so-and-so with a headache." To abandon that appendage now would be to change her self, or at least, and as an intermediary step, her self-image of her self. This was years before self psychology. I have thought of this insight in all the succeeding years in regard to difficult or stalled analyses, due to a failure, or inability, or unwillingness of the patient to alter his or her self identity—or at another level, in other cases, to endure what is felt as a self-castration. This spoken presentation remained one of my unpublished papers, not for lack of conviction, but because I could not give all my talks equal attention.

The same mechanism, perhaps even more easily, applies to fixed ideas, which are more ego-syntonic than symptoms and are therefore even more difficult to dislodge. An analyst, over years of training, indoctrination, and choices, at every level of consciousness, *becomes* a self psychologist, or a Kleinian, or a Freudian, or now the various combinations. He *is* that view; that *is* him. To Bergmann's concern that I overlook "the ferocity of the emotions" of those who hold dear their special theories, I not only do not deny these reactions but point to them, but I feel that they need to be understood. Why is there such ferocity or anathema to a suggested unification? At another point, Bergmann "would like to emphasize the word *understanding* [diversity and controversy]." But conditions are such that we should "not try to agree or form a consensus" (260), he states. I agree about seeking understanding. But analysts may/should go further, to go on from there if we can, to institutional action.

Bergmann and Richards both personally agree with the logical coherence of a unified theory while bowing to the intensity of those who oppose it. Renik (1997) says that everyone favors an integrated theory, but we do not yet have one. Smith (2005), after surveying thirteen contemporary views of conflict, states that we cannot live without theory. Yet, after quoting positively Haven's opinion in favor of pluralism of methods but not of theories, Smith argues for "a measure of imprecision" and states that we can integrate at the clinical level but not yet at the abstract. Listing many contradictions, incompatibilities, and non sequiturs in the variety of conflict theories, Smith writes, "I suggest that some of our best work stems from just such flaws" (351), which itself seems a flaw. "An overarching theory . . . is not yet written," he continues, and recommends a looser connection between theory and practice, a view he holds in common with Fonagy (2003). To me, the relationship between theory and practice is already loose, flexible, cooperative, and mutually helpful. Theory does not bind practice but guides it; the link between the two is open and continuously interdependent.

The ambiguity of the editor of the quarterly toward the subject of contemporary conflict that he assigned to be surveyed, stems, I suggest, from the same base that I attributed to Wallerstein (and secondarily to Sandler), that the editor of a major mainstream journal, or an officer, especially the president, of the major organization in our field, acquires the same mind-set in their positions of responsibility. The desideratum to leaders at the top is harmony. In this context, it is applied to equality of theories.

15

ONE THEORY, MANY TREATMENTS

WHICH IS IT?

In the meantime, there is a kaleidoscopic diversity. Within this, is it to be as Fenichel (1945) wrote, "There are many ways to treat neuroses but there is only one way to understand them" (554), that is, "one theory, many treatments," or "many understandings and one treatment" (in which the analytic treatment is the common ground), as Wallerstein, representing the opinions and pressures of many analysts, came to declare as the state of the field? This plural view of theory continues the idea of G. Klein on the original division of clinical from abstract theories. It was also the view of Sandler, in his final post–Anna Freud phase. Smith (2005) reluctantly concurs in the difficulty of a unification of theories, although he seems to feel differently but is resigned. In this view, I feel he speaks for most analysts.

Two opposite views of the current state of psychoanalytic theories, I would say, are operative in modern psychoanalytic life throughout the analytic world. One is that of Sandler (1983), who, in defense of divergent theories, writes that there is a discrepancy between public and private statements about the practice of analysis—that analysts commonly profess to be Freudian in public, while in private they find other theories more useful. While granting that this may be true, I (1990,

1997) have pointed out an opposite (and perhaps coexisting) inconsistency. Analysts commonly speak publicly about major divergences while privately finding long-standing Freudian concepts—objectivity, the use of transference in the original sense (as displacements from the past), the uncovering of unconscious conflicts, and interpretation and reconstruction—comfortably compatible with their practice of analysis. I feel that the basic intellectual tenets are survivors at least as much as the dissident views. In agreement with Fenichel, and I suspect with many who see the major aspects of early theory as permanent insights about the human condition, I feel in my daily psychoanalytic work that there is one total, cumulative, constantly advancing theory, and an infinite number of variations of the daily treatment strategies that derive from this overall understanding. The additions or special emphases that many creative analysts have discovered during the psychoanalytic century fit well into this total structure and would diminish understanding were they to replace this total view with these partial discoveries.

ANALYSTS RETURN TO THE MAIN PATH

In the same vein, analysts who ventured into other avenues return to the main field, or to conclusions compatible with it. Renik (1999), after a period considered by many as radical innovations, says that his changes in self-disclosure are made to the extent that they are in the patient's interest. To this, all can agree. Chused (1999), during the backlash of writings about enactment, says, "Now I am considered a 'classical analyst' because of my continuing belief in the utility of abstinence" (52). André Green (1993), as a discussant to the current flexible position of Ted Jacobs, stressing the role of the analyst and the use of the countertransference, takes a traditional position not unlike that which I (1975a) took toward him (Green) in the London debate of 1975. In that affective exchange, it was he who was stressing the new types of patients and methods, and I for conservation of the enduring frame. Greenberg (2001), a leading object-relations theorist, comes later to endorse drives. Schafer (1997), formerly a leading student and supporter of Rapaport, who later went on to a Kleinian position, sees modern Kleinians as close to contemporary Freudians.

Wallerstein (2000) himself now foresees a coming together of abstract theories. Kernberg (2001), who generally has positioned himself astride all theories, utilizing all quite freely, also foresees a "cross fertilization" and "a degree of convergence" in the future. In fact, I believe that perhaps all advocates of specific theories harbor a wish for or a belief in unity. Fonagy (2003), one of the most insistent authors in this field and a passionate defender of independence of theory, separating it from a strict guidance for practice, also warns in the strongest terms against multiple, partial theories. "This fragmentation, euphemistically characterized in the literature as pluralism, could potentially be fatal to psychoanalysis" (14). He is also surprisingly syntonic with my emphasis on adding without replacing. "The problem is rather one to claim exclusivity. . . . Thus, new ideas overlap with, but do not replace, the original formulation" (31).

Societies in several cities, split in the 1950s, merge in the 2000s. While some of these conversions are for pragmatic reasons, they nevertheless also bespeak a return to original concepts. In the meantime, those who never changed into the new directions are still regarded as reactionary or rigid. As the "premature antifascists" of the 1930s, the classical analysts who stayed that way were "right too soon"!

CONTROVERSIAL DISCUSSIONS VERSUS DISCUSSIONS OF CONTROVERSIES

Considering how regularly alternative psychoanalytic theories are built upon ideational fallacies and logical flaws, failing to take into account their continuing relationships to aspects of the previous theory they purportedly accept, it is striking how rare have been attempts at scientific reparation or efforts at retention of consistency and intellectual unity.

A notable exception, and historically the starting point for such an attempted rational exchange of differences, was the well-known Controversial Discussions of the British Society, conducted from 1941 to 1943, in the midst of the bombs dropping on London at the time. The aim was straightforward and rational, to attempt to confront directly the theoretical split in that society that was gaining momentum and dividing the analytic membership into opposite and contesting groups. As part of a series of "extraordinary business meetings" to consider the reorganization of the society, seven scientific meetings were held to discuss and attempt to resolve the widening theoretical differences between the Kleinian and Freudian positions that were splitting the society apart. With the best of intentions, the membership embarked on a rational approach to identify the differences involved and to compromise or otherwise resolve the conflicting ideas in a combined set of principles that would encompass and satisfy the views of both groups. The discussions, attended by probably the most creative cluster of analysts existing anywhere in the world at the time, have been documented by King and Steiner (1991) and studied by various others since then.

The results of these extended discussions, which were not salutary or logical or good for the field, were met with the same interpersonal and affective group inputs that contaminate such issues as I (2004) described in some detail as taking place in the following half century, as I experienced them firsthand during that time period (before that, I extrapolated retrospectively about what took place at the beginning and in the first half of the history of our field). Conflicts between the two major adversaries, Melanie Klein and Anna Freud and their followers, mingled with issues of power and dominance, obscured the theoretical differences, as much as each side tried to present their differing views as clearly as they could. Divergent opinions had developed between the two earliest child analysts about developmental factors in the first two years of life, and the clinical implications of these, at the time limited to child analysis but later to spill over to considerations of regressive symptomatology in adults as well. The contents of the arguments by this time could be seen to be a fusion of two streams, one an attempt to clarify scientific principles based on observations and theory formation, the other consisting of inputs stemming from affective, interpersonal links of the participants with and against the two leading figures.

Looking back at these discussions fifty years later, Reed and Baudry (1997), reporting for a study group that discussed these proceedings for two years, recount Anna Freud's initial attempt to expose the contradictions involved, and then her turning to the contested speculative positions that separated the two groups, which could not be resolved by observations or evidence but instead led to a stalemate of the discussion. The Kleinians, for their part, who felt threatened by expulsion, and whose ideas were argued mainly through a paper on fantasy by

Susan Isaacs, claimed an independent theory at the same time that they were declaring their position an extension of Freud's. Reed and Baudry, noting the opportunities as well as the failures, stated what should have been the fulcrum of the debates in a way that in my opinion applies to all other divergent theories before and since. Paraphrasing slightly, I cite three crucial questions: What clinical observations make the innovations necessary? Is the revision independent or does it link to or depend on some unrecognized aspect of previous theory? Does the new theory contradict some aspect of previous theory on which it silently depends?

Had such questions been systematically pursued and satisfied, some fusion might have been possible to retain a unified and coherent theory encompassing the acceptable new with the enduring old. As such, it could have been a model for future moments, or eras, of new innovations in theory and practice.

Instead, the discussions faltered, and the administrative compromise was put into effect that instituted a make-do scientific atmosphere in which three groups lived and trained under one umbrella, each alien to and variably critical of the other two. Also resulting was the resignation of Glover from the society (later rescinded) and Miss Freud from the training committee. I (2004) have described the further course of Anna Freud's ambivalent relationship with organized psychoanalysis, which in my opinion played a part in the international ascendancy of the Kleinian position that she intensely opposed.

Another official scientific discussion to compare competing theories took place in 1975 at the International Psychoanalytic Association Congress in London on "Changes in Psychoanalytic Theory and Practice." At the opening plenary session, the subject was discussed and debated between representatives of two continents, André Green and myself. Green, speaking for Europe and Great Britain, presented the changed scene: patients had become more disturbed and complex, psychopathology had moved far from Freud's early cases, neurotics or hysteria were not current fare—and the theory to deal with them had changed to a proportionate degree. Repression and the nuclear pathology of the Oedipus complex were insufficient explanations. Decathexis had replaced repression as the major mechanism of defense, and the here and now had become the locus of explanatory power over recovery of repressed memories. My position then, as since, officially representing the theoretical position of the American, was that theory had expanded to encompass the deeper psychopathology, that patients covered as wide a pathological span in Freud's time as they do now, that even the patients Freud treated had deeper psychopathology than he found then, and that "because we know more does not mean that patients are sicker." Green's theoretical view embraced the modern theorists of the time, Bion, Winnicott, Lacan, and Klein, the pluralism that existed at that period; mine was that the Freudian theoretical tree had extended to encompass a widened scope of patients (cf. Stone 1954).

I would not have included this debate as connected to the Controversial Discussions except that about a quarter century later, Martin Bergmann did just that. Writing in a celebration of the work of André Green, Bergmann (1999) resurrects this debate of 1975, referring to it as a landmark in the history of psychoanalysis, placing it in a series with earlier debates, on Ferenczi's active technique, Wilhelm Reich's character analysis, and the Controversial Discussions between the proponents of Melanie Klein and Anna Freud.

Bergmann's conclusions, however, in a later era of much-expanded pluralism, are quite the opposite of mine and perhaps give a clue as to the nature of the preference by the mass of analysts for the new and puzzling over the old and clear. "In the debate itself, Rangell and Anna Freud [who was the discussant of the two papers] carried the day," Bergmann writes, but he goes on to suggest that "the era they represented had already passed" (198–99). Noting approvingly Green's creative work on the negative, on psychic space and the dead mother, and the move from ego defenses toward object-relations, Bergmann supports "the deadly power of decathexis as a fundamental alternative to repression" (196). This debate, Bergmann points out, occurred just as psychoanalytic theory exploded from a fairly uniform system to a cluster of competing theories. The analytic center, "so eloquently defended by Rangell and Anna Freud, could not turn back the tide of change that André Green had represented" (203). Although winning "hands down" on contents—that is, cognition and logic—the arguments presented by Rangell and Anna Freud bear no relation to affecting the tides of change, Bergmann notes, without opposing but implicitly approving this contradiction.

Bergmann repeats and expands in further writings his ambivalence toward the expanded ego theory that I was already describing in 1975. In the symposium on understanding controversy and dissidence that I referred to above, Bergmann (2004) again expressed doubt on my effort and method to unify and extend Freudian theory, feeling that it was only my own vision as to what would be included and left out that I would countenance. This is not my intended method. Why not a "Discussion of Controversy" in which each item—repression, the structural view, decathexis, recovered memories—is examined separately on its merits, and decisions on each are made by consenting compromises of all the contesting participants?

In the absence of such efforts, an irregular group of concepts is either highlighted or discarded by a varied group of partial theorists, while a synthesis is sought by affective harmony without any discussion of specific concepts. André Green, in fact, one of the invited participants in Bergmann's modern-day symposium, accepts "a widespread dissent . . . [as] just realistic. . . . Taking it too seriously would lead to minute splitting, war, and death. . . . It is too late for regrets" (126–27). Bergmann himself states that he wishes not to repeat the difficulties of the Controversial Discussions of the British Society, but he finds his efforts not able to avoid them (262). Perhaps our combined efforts can one day cooperate in achieving this aim.

A consequence of the void in discussion is the passive acceptance of contradictions and inconsistencies. Perhaps the sheer volume of the contents of the field, and even the profusion of the literature attempting to encompass it, defies any significant attempt to bring order and logic. It would be a leap forward were controversial discussions now followed by discussions of controversies—in a good sense.

A CURRENT SUMMARY OF THE FIELD

In a recent article, Kernberg (2001) summarizes, in a didactic, outline form, without indicating his own choices or preferences, characteristics of the major technical approaches in use today deriving from the theoretical schools of thought acceptable in the modern psychoanalytic world. Examining the competing orientations over the past fifty years,

Kernberg essentially traverses the same ground as I have, except as information only, devoid of a history of the reasons or methods behind developments that evolved, and without an attempt to choose some concepts and reject or downplay others. Thorough and broad, leaving it open to every reader to decide and choose for himself, this rather superordinate presentation can be said to replicate the present ambience of pluralism, encouraging an even disposition to all theories and assuming that the methods by which each was conceived and developed had equal validity. Regardless of what Kernberg himself finds to be the most compatible theory or combination for his own use and taste, this listing in essence duplicates the present atmosphere in which the theory of psychoanalysis resides. As such, it permits recognition of some of the overlaps, conflicts, incompatibilities, and limitations of the range of views.

This overall view can serve us well, presenting the analytic world, in the opinion of one of its most prominent representatives, as it is, not as it should or can be, at least in the opinion of some. In an educational mode, Kernberg explains that psychoanalytic theory today is divided into three major streams, two in the English-speaking world, and the third a unique approach of the French school. The two dominant English-speaking theories today consist of "the psychoanalytic mainstream—derived from contemporary Kleinian, contemporary Freudian, and British independent sources, and the intersubjective-interpersonal-self psychology current" (519). The third is the idiosyncratic French approach to psychoanalytic technique.

After describing the tenets of the original three British divisions, which he identifies as the beginning of the contemporary developments in psychoanalytic technique, Kernberg is most impressed with "the gradual rapprochement of these 3 viewpoints" by a new generation of analysts (522). Starting on a base of the British "gentleman's agreement" at the conclusion of their Controversial Discussions, Kernberg combines the three divisions that resulted, brought up to date as their contemporary versions, with American ego psychology, to create a new "English-speaking mainstream." The new dominant current thus is the alliance of contemporary Freud and modern Klein, along with the British middle group and ego psychology. The assumption or assertion is that such a global fusion is a working unit today. This formulation makes the traditional, historical mainstream that I described—that is, ego psychology, with the ego overseeing the rest of the personality—no longer the "main one," which has now been replaced.

The fact is, in my opinion, that no such combined theory is in force today, but the divisive boundaries that originally separated groups continue to exist in less vivid or overt ways in the modern psychoanalytic world. A Kleinian is still a Kleinian, and a relationist or intersubjectivist remains steeped in that tradition and set of convictions. Close attention to the characteristics of each division provided with such precision by Kernberg reveals the same disarray as before, a field replete with inconsistencies, non sequiturs, historical misrepresentations, misattributions, and omissions, which multiply as Kernberg's detailed descriptions proceed to demonstrate the central tenets of each theoretical group. It is conspicuous that these are listed in a running stream virtually without comment. The differences and inconsistencies are strengthened by a seemingly quiet acceptance.

I will point to a few of these illogicalities, paradigmatic of others, to view their inner inconsistencies and passive acceptance of contradictions. I will do this not as germane to Kernberg's own operative theoretical body, but as reflecting the attitudes of the general psychoanalytic population to the current pluralistic ambience. For Kernberg, in my opinion, portrays accurately the overall mental set toward the state of current thinking and its generally passive acceptance of contradictions and lack of coherence within its total theoretical corpus.

Describing the contemporary Kleinian position, Kernberg states that Rosenfeld, by applying Kleinian technique to narcissistic patients, and Steiner by applying it to pathological personality disorders, extended Kleinian technique to character disorders (523). But character is not synonymous with narcissism or personality disorder; it applies to the spectrum of personality traits, from benign to disturbed. Was this contribution the crossing of a previous gap, or was it an evolution in technique? And did it separate one school from another? Did traditional Klein exempt character disorders from Kleinian analysis (waiting for Rosenfeld to accomplish this)? Did ego psychology learn something new from this extension? Had they also ignored character pathology? Where do Wilhelm Reich's contributions fit in?

Or, Kernberg states, "Mainstream Kleinians changed from concern with anatomical organs to stress primitive fantasies." Was there such a discernible change? Do not both inhabit the Kleinian world, early and late and still? Are not all analysts concerned with all unconscious fantasies, primitive or more "advanced"? Or, he also states, "Interpretations became less categorical, less focused on aggression and envy, and more attuned to the dominant level of anxiety in the here and now" (523). This is how ego psychology always worked. So, have Kleinians now become synonymous with ego psychology, from which these methods are no different?

Continuing his descriptive review, he states, "Simultaneously, within the contemporary Freudian approach, a number of analysts in Great Britain . . . began to include an object relations perspective in their theoretical formulations and technical interventions" (524). Were these two not always together in routine, total psychoanalytic theory? Did this move create anything new or change anything? Kernberg quotes the Sandlers' change in emphasis to object-relations without any reference to facts about external contributions to this era of change (this shift occurring following the death of Anna Freud). The Sandlers "stressed the central importance of affects" (525), another re-find of a regular emphasis. "A new mainstream of analytic technique within the English-language community seems to be evolving" (525), Kernberg writes.

The French approach is the third major contemporary stream—the International groups, separate from the Lacanian—whose main tenets Kernberg lists, many of them brief summary statements of questionable logic. Described are the linguistic aspects: the downplaying of transference and of cognitive interpretations (How is this done? Interpretations are in ideational terms, though of course to be delivered with appropriate affect); direct interpretations of psychosomatic manifestations (the "school" of Pierre Marty) (Is this the preferred route over verbal communications?); and, respecting the "irreducible basis of earliest transferences," the mother's enigmatic early messages (the contribution of Laplanche) (cf. Leo Stone's archaic defenses, also a limiting factor of the analytic reach). Are specific contributions of French analysts any more to be considered schools than the multitude of individual authors in the English-speaking groups? Is the analytic method in France via the soma rather than by verbal communication any more by shared affect than by understanding? Can this be within the paradigm of psychoanalysis?

Kernberg's listing of the major concepts of each theoretical stream as they are grouped today, and the contents of each, permits a clear view of the ambiguities that exist, and of the need to make definitive choices to achieve clarity and coherence. This didactic listing of current theoretical beliefs, an authentic summary by a recognized leading educator, represents not just the view of the individual author but reflects well the operative opinion of the psychoanalytic public toward the potpourri of schools active in today's psychoanalytic world. I would add to this milieu that this generally held inventory of the similarities and differences between schools, and of the directions being traveled, also contains within it an unconscious appreciation of the original formulations and values, and of which deviations create diversions and divisiveness. However beset with resistances and inhibitions, I wish to express a confidence in the unconscious insights of a widespread psychoanalytic public. This is why I believe that, within the multitude of theories and therapies extant in the intellectual world of Western civilization today, automatic homage is paid to the superordinacy of Freudian theory as the progenitor of them all. And that is why I opt for a view that sees many treatments but one theory. The multitiered and complex maze of the one psychoanalytic tree of knowledge encompasses human behavior, with room for the unknown as well.

As a sign toward this deeper knowledge, in the midst of his descriptions of the many corrective movements countering the traditional, objectivistic view of the analyst's role, after listing the myriad, diverging contents and the changes toward amalgamation that he perceives, Kernberg intersperses, "All of these developments moved Kleinian analysis in the direction of ego psychology, without explicit acknowledgement of this shift" (523). Which theory is total, and enduring, and can absorb and contain the contributions of others is quite clear, even though this is not readily acknowledged. Many know this only in the deepest layers, only unconsciously. Providing another example of unconscious insight, which has trouble being overt, after a detailed, seemingly value-free listing, Kernberg concludes, "I have suggested ways in which each of [the current streams] may be flawed and incomplete" (543). That more insight lives than is acknowledged is why I suggest that many analysts practice many theories while deeply calling on the Freudian base for their ultimate beliefs—rather than the reverse, paying homage to traditional theory while believing in the dissident ones.

In the end, Kernberg sees a "cross-fertilization during the past 30 years . . . a trend toward mutual modification of previously hotly defended differences [from which, if it continues], one might expect a degree of convergence in the French and English schools in the years to come" (543). No more concrete facts are presented to back this hope than is given by Wallerstein in seeing a future reunion of abstract theories. Bergmann (2004) "does not trust history alone to achieve this aim" (96). Neither do I. But not because multiple theories are not taught respectfully, as Bergmann fears, but because a method of unification has not been accepted or agreed upon generally. I believe that beyond mutual respect, which is essential, the field must be ready for discussions, comparisons, rational choices, and realistic compromises.

A serendipitous observation has come my way in researching the period of the Flexner report, which I described above, that has an unexpected relevance to my current theme. "The great mass of the public," declared the medical educator John Shaw Billings in 1891, "know little and care less about the details of professional education. . . . The popular feeling is that in a free country every one should have the right to follow any occupation he likes, and employ for any purpose any one whom he selects, and that each party must take the consequences. . . . We teach all theories equally. The candidates choose" (Billings 1891). This dilemma in medicine at the turn of the century resonates to the stance of institutes of psychoanalysis today. "We teach all theories. The candidates then choose," is exactly the inducement in the catalogs of many a modern institute leafed through by those considering training in psychoanalysis today.

16

MY ADDITIONS

MY ADDITIONS TO THE TOTAL THEORY

I have added my own contributions to developing theory during these decades. Without details, I would like to summarize and help organize these additions into several categories.

One is in the terrain of psychoanalysis and dynamic psychotherapy, similarities and differences, the separations and the overlaps. I entered this field in the first panel of the American on this subject in 1954 and have participated in numerous follow-up symposia throughout the next five decades in programs of both the American and the International associations.

A second overall topic is that of unconscious choice and decision making. I added the unconscious decision-making function to the inventory of ego functions in the 1960s and 1970s. The focus of these writings was on "the active unconscious ego," later "the executive functions of the ego." These led to a psychoanalytic theory of action, which both Hartmann and Rapaport had declared missing from psychoanalytic theory.

Choice or dilemma conflicts, the necessity to make either-or decisions, were added to oppositional conflicts, such as the routine or traditional conflict between the ego and the id. This is a stage in the intrapsychic sequence during the ubiquitous unconscious process of testing for anxiety preceding external outcomes. Following receipt of the signal of either anxiety or safety, the next intrapsychic move is to set into motion the active "unconscious decision-making function" of the ego, which leads, among other modes of resolution of conflict, to choice between alternatives, compromise formations (the latter also involves choice of compromise), or autonomous acts.

The latter is the base for the realm of creativity. Aside from Anton Kris (1977, 1984) having taken up this subject again in the late 1970s and 1980s, in the form of convergent and divergent conflicts, the consequences of this addition have not been assimilated into general psychoanalytic theory. As unconscious choice needs to be added to compromise formations to explain the myriad of external psychic outcomes, the same psychic function has been minimized in the history of the development of theory. Not every move, external or intrapsychic, is a compromise; many require choice. This applies as well to competing theories. Often, the choice is between alternative compromises.

Embedded at this juncture of unconscious intrapsychic activity is the operation of "relatively free will." A concept is introduced that adds a psychoanalytic view to the age-old philosophic subject of free will. Freud discovered psychic determinism, which cast a new dimension on this conundrum of perpetual debate. While this was a major addition, however, it is not a total explanation of the motive power of behavior. Determinism shares the stage with autonomy in the field of action. Unconscious ego will plays a part, but it is only relatively free. After considering the forces that impinge on man in his daily life, from within and without, I (1986) suggested the conclusion, "Human history, individual and collective, results from a combination of determinism, random occurrences, and the guided event" (30). From another perspective, that of determinism, freedom, and democracy, "Life is a combination of what has to be, and what we make of that" (Rangell 2004, 314).

Parallel to the newly described conflicts of the ego, other writings pointed to conflicts at the ego's other flank, its surface toward the superego. From data coming from the external world of human political life, as well as from group interrelations within the field of psychoanalysis itself, both supplemented by cumulated clinical experiences, I (1974, 1976, 1980) described "the syndrome of the compromise of integrity" as "on a par with neuroses in human affairs." Conflicts between the ego and the superego are as ubiquitous as conflicts between the ego and the id, although psychoanalysis, in its clinical focus, has had more opportunities to study the latter.

Advancing from Hartmann's (1958) and Waelder's (1960) classic positions that moral conflicts are outside the domain of psychoanalytic interest or interpretations, a neutral stance in keeping with the historical era establishing the aim and method of psychoanalysis, moral conflicts can also now be seen as dysfunctional states that can be subject to analysis, understanding, and influence. Phenomenologically, such pathology is increasingly pressing and invasive and can hardly be turned away from. In the therapeutic process, moral as well as instinctual conflicts, as with all conflicts, are to be treated analytically, not moralistically. The aim is the same as for neuroses: exposure of the unconscious operations around anxiety and providing insight to help produce results. The obstacles as well as the possibilities are well known and exist across the spectrum of diagnoses. The degree of difficulty in the two syndromes—symptoms or pathological behavior from either the id or the superego pressing the ego—is relative. Of course, the method has little or no application in extreme conditions along either line. But where it is relevant, analysis, in its total effect, should produce more honest as well as less neurotic individuals.

With these additions, the question of responsibility acquires a new complexity. While from the traditional advance of early theory man was less responsible than he thought, because of the newly discovered unconscious motivation, he is now at the same time more responsible than he knows, because of unconscious decisions and actions he actively brings about, of which he is as unconscious as of his repressed motives. Both dynamics exist together.

Surrounding these new foci of unconscious activity, a spine running through my orientation about the functioning of the mental apparatus is a concept that started from Freud's process testing for signal anxiety, which I developed further from there in stages. First, studying the structural view (Rangell 1963a, 1963b) and pursuing the "microdynamics" of the signal process, I pointed to "unconscious intrapsychic conflicts" as delineating the pathognomonic area separating the terrain of psychoanalysis from that of other social sciences. Recognizing further that not all "trial actions" encounter unconscious conflicts, some presaging safety rather than eliciting anxiety, a wider concept became "the unconscious intrapsychic process." Freud's unconscious signal process is dissected into some fourteen steps that precede every intended act, searching for expectable consequences as tested against previous traumatic states. I (1967, 1990) identified and named this area and its functioning as "the human core."

Within this core process, castration anxiety (Rangell 1991) is given its due place and is not permitted to decline in attention. Of the two primary anxieties of human life, castration and separation anxieties, separation, in connection with its counterpart of attachment, has occupied a dominant position, in contrast to the role of castration anxiety, which has receded and is not heard much today in clinical or life accounts. This is no indication, however, of the major unconscious role it continues to play in both individual and collective psychopathology, in neuroses, and in recurrent wars and increasing incidents of mass terror. From a waning interest in this etiologic influence comes a distorted and incomplete understanding of gender identity problems, perversions, and the place of sexuality in general in human psychology and psychopathology. Many of the alternative, interpersonal theories encourage this diminution of emphasis.

Another thrust of my writings has been toward a unification of theory. An early subject along this line had to do with Freud's two theories of anxiety. Freud himself, when he introduced his second, revised theory, was left puzzled about the fate of his first theory and the relationship between the two. At the end, he concluded that "non liquet"—that is, the two do not flow together—but he could not discard the first as he added the second. In two papers, in 1955 and 1968, I offered a unified theory of anxiety, combining Freud's two theories, ending with "now liquet." The first was part of a physiological explanation, the second the psychological; both applied and worked together. In the next three decades, I (culminating in Rangell 2004) wrote of a unified, cumulative "total composite psychoanalytic theory," which offers a fusion of all the dissident theories that have plagued the field and kept it fragmented since the beginning.

Psychoanalytic theory stems from individual observations but applies on the widest scale. Its insights can be directed wherever human psychology plays a part. I have always maintained an interest in group psychology and the equal role it plays with individual psychology in cultural and mass psychopathology. This led to my work on the role of the electorate in the national Nixon-Watergate experience, and to my describing the ubiquitous "syndrome of the compromise of integrity" as seen in group life. Supplementing the common pointing to malignant leaders, I (1981a) have written on "leaders and led" and have stressed the role and contribution of the base of the population pyramid in determining outcomes and the directions of mass movements. Untoward outcomes, from mild to severe, up to wars and the horrors of the Holocaust, cannot take place without the complicity of the populace in each instance, even if by their silent participation.

Included in this group application of the knowledge that comes from psychoanalytic theory is my work (2005) on the psychology of public opinion. As a sequel to Freud's group psychology, I (2004) have shown that mass psychology is subject to the same explanatory system as the psychology of the individual. Psychoanalytic theory is applicable and operative in all large mass experiences, or incidents in which large numbers take part, wherever human reactions count, such as public reactions to major crimes, sensational trials, elections, appointments of Supreme Court justices, national traumata, and geographic catastrophes, including tornados, floods, fires, hurricanes, and tsunamis. The insights of depth psychology also help to understand reverse outcomes, like the idolization and cultish following of celebrities, beauty, and aggressive behavior.

Alternative theories do not have the inside track to widespread applicability; traditional theory, when complete, has an equal reach. Psychoanalysis, as a total theory, has more relevance than we have yet come to imagine or set about to explore. The core of unconscious human mental activity, whether one thinks of it as the infantile neurosis or the signal process for anxiety, is enduring throughout the history of psychoanalytic theory. At the same time, both it and the periphery to the external world remain open to change in their entire circumference. The mental apparatus, whether of an individual or an abstract collective, is subject to continuous modification based on new inputs from the widest external surround.

17

UNITY AND RECONCILIATION WITHIN PSYCHOANALYSIS

THE PRESENT AND FUTURE

Theory is suspect. Interest in theory remains inconstant and ambivalent. "What's the difference?" one often hears; "What is this fuss all about, making so much of theories?" "We take what we can from each theory," say those who feel positive about the current pluralism. Theodore Reik (1948), who rightly pointed to the casual third ear as the important receptor of meaningful messages of the patient, argued with Fenichel (1941) that theory leads to an overemphasis of intellect and ideation at the expense of affects, which are the lifeblood of the analytic interchange. Years later, the same position was taken by Fonagy (2003), arguing that theories constrain, that analysts do better free of such constrictions, which are used as superego criticisms of those who deviate from accepted theory. This is not unlike the spirit and admonitions of Bion (1970), against memory and desire, and the many who support him affectively in feeling this.

But again we see the operation of the parts for the whole, of one pole of a pair being demolished, of the neglect of the complemental series. Intellectualization as a defense is misinterpreted as against the use of intellect. During the heyday of ego psychology, some thought that the ego replaced the id. The fact is that, with insistent regularity, in all of these pairs, both poles apply; only both of each pair together constitute and round out the whole. Ideation and affects, id and ego, theory and the freedom to change it—they all live together. Ideas and affects reside within analysis, both as subjects and as parts of the analyzing instrument, although in different proportions. Theory is not restrictive of observations; it in fact demands them. Fonagy, as did Sandler (1983) before him, stresses the operation of each analyst's private theories, as though these are frowned upon, or forbidden, and contrary to "public" ones. Such theories, hunches, preinterpretations, and nascent or pretheories are indeed present and useful, by every analyst, in every hour. There is nothing inimical between public and private theories. Public theories are those that have achieved a degree of consensus.

Turning to the body of abstract theory that has accumulated incrementally over the century, Shevrin (2003), pointing to the same circumstances in the 1960s that I recounted when a section of the Topeka group turned away from Rapaport's systematizing formulations, writes of "the consequences of abandoning a comprehensive psychoanalytic theory." "Revisiting Rapaport's 'The Structure of Psychoanalytic Theory: A Systematizing Attempt,'" Shevrin writes that as a result, "Psychoanalysis as a science and practice is in grave danger of conceptual rootlessness. . . . The development of a cumulative body of evidence once well underway has essentially come to a halt" (1019). I can add that the present decline and malaise, of which so many, inside and outside the field, are conscious today, were furthered by the same theoretical distancing from Freud, Hartmann, Anna Freud, Fenichel, and others, upon whose collective work such a coherent, composite system, worthy of being included in the family of science, was built.

A total, composite unitary theory, developed by accretion, aiming at completeness with parsimony, constitutes such a coherent and comprehensive theory of psychoanalysis. After a century of having been applied clinically and on the widest psychosocial sphere, its ingredients, at its central unconscious core and in its wider ramifications, hold up as an explanatory theoretical system fitting to the data to which they are directed. The path to coherence is the road to unity. Countering its contemporary status, in which a total, cumulative theory is passively avoided, or actively resisted, such a comprehensive integration of partial theories can lead to unity and reconciliation in a now-fragmented psychoanalysis. A resumption of the incremental theoretical development and steady advances made quietly even during periods of decline may reinstate the inspirational quality enjoyed by psychoanalysis during its peak years.

BIBLIOGRAPHY

Beck, A. H. 2004. Flexner report and the standardization of American medical education. *JAMA* 291:2139–40.

Bergmann, M. 1999. The dynamics of the history of psychoanalysis: Anna Freud, Leo Rangell, and André Green. In *The dead mother: The work of André Green*, ed. Gregorio Kohon, 193–204. New York: Routledge.

———, ed. 2000. *The Hartman Era*. New York: Other Press.

———. 2004. *Understanding dissidence and controversy in the history of psychoanalysis*. New York: Other Press.

Billings, J. S. 1891. Ideals of medical education. *Science* 18:1–4.

Bion, W. R. 1970. *Attention and interpretation*. New York: Basic Books.

Brenner, C. 1999. Reflections on psychoanalysis. Paper delivered to the New York Psychoanalytic Society, June 13.

Bronstein, A. 2005. Re: money and pharmaceuticals. Openline, Amer. Psychoanal. Assn., July 16.

Brooks, P., and A. Woloch. 2000. *Whose Freud? The place of psychoanalysis in contemporary culture*. New Haven, CT: Yale Univ. Press.

Chused, J. F. 1999. Four aspects of the enactment concept: Definitions; therapeutic effects; dangers; history. *J. Clin. Psychoanal.* 8:9–62.

El Hai, J. 2005. *The lobotomist: A maverick medical genius and his tragic quest to rid the world of mental illness*. Hoboken, NJ: John Wiley & Sons.

Ellman, C. S., S. Grand, M. Silvan, and S. J. Ellman, eds. 1998. *The modern Freudians: Contemporary psychoanalytic technique*. Northvale, NJ: Jason Aronson Inc.

Fenichel, O. 1941. *Problems of psychoanalytic technique*. New York: *Psychoanal. Q.*

———. 1945. *The psychoanalytic theory of neurosis*. New York: Norton.

Flexner, A. 1910. Medical education in the United States and Canada. New York: Carnegie Foundation for the Advancement of Teaching.

Fonagy, P. 2003. Some complexities in the relationship of psychoanalytic theory to technique. *Psychoanal. Q.* 72:13–47.

———. Complexities in the relation of theory to technique. *Psychoanal. Q.* 42: 13–47.

Fonagy, P., H. Kachele, R. Krause, E. Jones, R. Person, J. Clarkin, A. J. Gerber, and E. Allison. 2001. *An open door review of outcome studies in psychoanalysis*. Int. Psychoanal. Assn.

Fonagy, P., M. Target, G. Gergely, and E. J. Jurist. 2002. *Affect regulation, mentalization and the development of the self*. New York: Other Press.

Freud, A. 1936. *The ego and the mechanisms of defense*. New York: Int. Univ. Press, 1946.

———. Acting out. *Int. J. Psycho-Anal.* 49: 165–70.

Freud, S. 1895. Project for a scientific psychology. *S.E.* 1.

———. 1897. Letter 96. In *The Origins of psychoanalysis: Letters, drafts and notes to Wilhelm Fliess (1887–1902)*. New York: Basic Books.

———. 1900. The interpretation of dreams. *S.E.* 4 and 5.

———. 1901. The psychopathology of everyday life. *S.E.* 6.

———. 1905a. Three essays on the theory of sexuality. *S.E.* 7.

———. 1905b. Jokes and their relation to the unconscious. *S.E.* 8.

———. 1913. Totem and taboo. *S.E.* 13.

———. 1915. Five metapsychological points of view. *S.E.* 14.

———. 1920. Beyond the pleasure principle. *S.E.* 18.

———. 1921. Group psychology and the analysis of the ego. *S.E.* 18.

———. 1923. The ego and the id. *S.E.* 19.

———. 1926a. Inhibitions, symptoms and anxiety. *S.E.* 20.

———. 1926b. The question of lay analysis. *S.E.* 20

———. 1927. Concluding remarks on the question of lay analysis. *Int. J. Psycho-Anal.* 8:392–401.

———. 1933. New introductory lectures on psychoanalysis. *S.E.* 22.

Freud, S., and E. Jones. 1908–1939. *The complete correspondence of Sigmund Freud and Ernest Jones*, ed. R. Andrew Paskauskas. Cambridge: Belknap Press of Harvard University Press, 1993.

Gerard, R. W. 1959. Neurophysiology. In *American handbook of psychiatry*, vol. 7, ed. S. Arieti, 1620–38. New York: Basic Books.

Gill, M. M. 1954. Psychoanalysis and exploratory psychotherapy. *J. Amer. Psychoanal. Assn.* 2:771–97.

———. 1967. In memoriam: David Rapaport, 1911–1960. In *The collected papers of David Rapaport*, ed. M. M. Gill, 3–7. New York: Basic Books.

———. 1984. Psychoanalysis and psychotherapy: 1954–1979. Atlanta, October 20, Psychoanalysis and psychotherapy: A revision. *Int. Rev. of Psychoanal.* 11:161–80.

Glover, E. 1955. The therapeutic effect of inexact interpretation: A contribution to the theory of suggestion. In *The technique of psychoanalysis*, 353–66. New York: Int. Univ. Press.

Gray, P. 2000. On the receiving end. *J. Amer. Psychoanal. Assn.* 48:219–36.

Green, A. 1975. The analyst, symbolization and absence in the analytic setting (on changes in analytic practice and analytic experience)—in memory of D. W. Winnicott. *Int. J. Psycho-Anal.* 56:1–22.

———. 1993. Discussion of Jacobs, T. 38th International Psychoanalytic Congress, Amsterdam, Holland.

———. 2005. The illusion of common ground and mythical pluralism. *Int. J. Psycho-Anal.* 86:627–32.

Greenacre, P. 1963. *The quest for the father: A study of the Darwin-Butler controversy, as a contribution to the understanding of the creative individual*. New York: Int. Univ. Press.

Greenberg, J. 2001. The analyst's participation: A new look. *J. Amer. Psychoanal. Assn.* 49:359–81.

Grotstein, J. S. 1981. Seminar, Los Angeles Psychoanalytic Society and Institute.

Hall, J. 2005. Openline, Amer. Psychoanal. Assn., March 24.

Hartmann, H. 1958. *Ego psychology and the problem of adaptation*. Trans. David Rapaport. New York: Int. Univ. Press.

Horney, K. 1937. *The neurotic personality of our time*. New York: Norton.

Jacoby, R. 1986. (Quoted in A.7. Schneider and H. Desmond, 1994, below.)

Kernberg, O. F. 1982. Self, ego, affects, and drives. *J. Amer. Psychoanal. Assn.* 30:893–917.

———. 2001. Recent developments in the technical approaches of English-language psychoanalytic schools. *Psychoanal. Q.* 70:519–47.

Kety, S. S. 1960. A biologist examines the mind and behavior. *Science* 132:1861.

King, P., and R. Steiner. 1991. *The Freud-Klein controversies 1941–45*. New York: Routledge.

Klein, G. S. 1973. Two theories or one? *Bull. Menninger Clin.* 37:102–32.

Kohut, H. 1971. *The analysis of the self.* New York: Int. Univ. Press.

———. 1977. *The restoration of the self.* New York: Int. Univ. Press.

Kris, A. O. 1977. Either-or dilemmas. *The Psychoanal. Study of the Child* 32:91–117.

———. 1984. The conflicts of ambivalence. *The Psychoanal. Study of the Child* 39:213–34.

Kris, E. 1936. The psychology of caricature. *Int. J. Psycho-Anal.*, 17:285–303.

Loewald, H. 1960. On the therapeutic action of psycho-analysis. *Int. J. Psycho-Anal.* 41:16–33.

Neutzel, E. J. 2005. The soul of our association. *The American Psychoanalyst* 39 (3): 5, 36.

Perlman, F. 2005. Personal communication.

Rangell, L. 1954a. Similarities and differences between psychoanalysis and dynamic psychotherapy. *J. Amer. Psychoanal. Assn.* 2:734–44.

———. 1954b. A tertiary gain of symptoms. Paper read at the meeting of the Amer. Psychoanal. Assn., New York.

———. 1955a. On the psychoanalytic theory of anxiety: A statement of a unitary theory. *J. Amer. Psychoanal. Assn.* 3:389–414.

———. 1955b. The quest for ground in human motivation. Paper presented at a meeting of the West Coast Psychoanalytic Societies, San Francisco, October 29.

———. 1963a. The scope of intrapsychic conflict: Microscopic and macroscopic considerations. *Psychoanal. Study of the Child* 18:75–102.

———. 1963b. Structural problems in intrapsychic conflict. *Psychoanal. Study of the Child* 18:103–38.

———. 1967. Psychoanalysis, affects, and the "human core"—on the relationship of psychoanalysis to the behavioral sciences. *Psychoanal. Q.* 36:172–202.

———. 1968. A further attempt to resolve "the problem of anxiety." *J. Amer. Psychoanal. Assn.* 16:371–404.

———. 1971. Obituary, Dr. Heinz Hartmann. 134th Bull. Int. Psychoanal. Assn., *Int. J. Psycho-Anal.* 51:567.

———. 1974. A psychoanalytic perspective leading currently to the syndrome of the compromise of integrity. *Int. J. Psycho-Anal.* 55:3–12.

———. 1975a. Psychoanalysis and the process of change. *Int. J. Psycho-Anal.* 56:87–98.

———. 1975b. Man in a group. Address to the Third Robert Waelder Memorial Lecture, Philadelphia Association for Psychoanalysis, October 17.

———. 1975c. Book review of the Freud/Jung Letters, ed. W. McGuire,

Bollingen Series 94, trans. by Ralph Manheim and R. F. C. Hull. *Amer. J. Psychiat.* 132:980.

———. 1976. Lessons from Watergate: A derivative for psychoanalysis. *Psychoanal. Q.* 45:37–61.

———. 1980. *The mind of Watergate: An exploration of the compromise of integrity*. New York: W. W. Norton.

———. 1981a. Leaders and led: From official politics to psychoanalytic group life. Congress summary: Statements by leaders of special discussion groups. 32nd Int. Psychoanal. Cong., Helsinki, July 30, p. 51.

———. 1981b. Psychoanalysis and dynamic psychotherapy: Similarities and differences twenty-five years later. *Psychoanal. Q.* 50:665–93.

———. 1982. Transference to theory: The relationship of psychoanalytic education to the analyst's relationship to psychoanalysis. *Ann. Psychoanal.* 10:29–56.

———. 1986. The executive functions of the ego: An extension of the concept of ego autonomy. *Psychoanal. Study of the Child* 41:1–37.

———. 1988. The future of psychoanalysis: The scientific crossroads. *Psychoanal. Q.* 57:313–40.

———. 1989. Action theory within the structural view. *Int. J. Psycho-Anal.* 70:189–203.

———. 1990. *The human core: The intrapsychic base of behavior*. Vol. 1, *Action within the structural view*. Vol. 2, *From anxiety to integrity*. Madison, CT: Int. Univ. Press.

———. 1991. Castration. *J. Amer. Psychoanal. Assn.*, 39:3–23.

———. 1997. Into the second psychoanalytic century: One psychoanalysis or many? The unitary theory of Leo Rangell, M.D. *J. Clin. Psychoanal.* 6 (4): 451–612.

———. 1998. Psychoanalysis at the millennium: A unitary theory. *Samiksa, Journal of the Indian Psychoanalytical Society* 2:1–12. Also in *Psychoanal. Psychology* 17 (Summer 2000): 451–66.

———. 2000. Psyche and soma: Leaps and continuities. *J. Clin. Psychoanal.* 9:173–200.

———. Psychoanalytic psychotherapy: The enduring legacy of Psychoanalysis. *Psychoanal. Review* 88: 1–14.

———. 2002. Discussion of Brenner's "Reflections on Psychoanalysis"—and parallel reflections. *J. Clin. Psychoanal.* 11:96–114.

———. 2004. *My life in theory*. New York: Other Press.

———. 2005. The psychoanalysis of public opinion: The public as jury. *Psychoanal. Psychology* 22:3–20.

Rapaport, D., and M. M. Gill. 1959. The points of view and assumptions of metapsychology. *Int. J. Psycho-Anal.* 40:153–62.

Reed, G. S., and F. Baudry. 1997. Susan Isaacs and Anna Freud on fantasy. *J. Amer. Psychoanal. Assn.* 45:465–90.

Reichmayr, J., and E. Muhlleitner., eds. 1998. *Otto Fenichel: 119 Rundbriefe (1934–1945).* 2 vols. Frankfurt and Basel: Stroemfeld Verlag.

Reik, T. 1948. *Listening with the third ear.* New York: Farrar, Straus.

Renik, O. 1993. Analytic interaction: Conceptualizing technique in light of the analyst's irreducible subjectivity. *Psychoanal. Q.* 62:553–71.

———. 1996. The perils of neutrality. *Psychoanal. Q.* 65:495–517.

———. 1997. Discussion remarks (in Rangell 1997, above).

———. 1999. Four aspects of the enactment concept: Definitions; therapeutic effects; dangers; history. *J. Clin. Psychoanal.* 8:9–62.

Richards, A. D. 1999. A. A. Brill and the politics of exclusion. *J. Amer. Psychoanal. Assn.* 47:9–28.

———. 2000. A plea for a measure of humility: Psychoanalytic discourse at the turn of our century. Unpublished manuscript.

———. 2005a. Openline, Amer. Psychoanal. Assn., March 24.

———. 2005b. Personal communication, July 20.

Richards, A. D., and A. A. Lynch. 1998. From ego psychology to contemporary conflict theory: An historical overview. In C. S. Ellman, S. Grand, M. Silvan, and S. J. Ellman, eds., *The modern Freudians: Contemporary psychoanalytic technique.* Northvale, NJ: Jason Avonson, 1998: 3–23.

Sachs, D. 2005. Openline, Amer. Psychoanal. Assn., March 31.

Sandler, J. 1983. Reflections on some relations between psychoanalytic concepts and psychoanalytic practice. *Int. J. Psycho-Anal.* 64:35–45.

Sandler, J., and A. Freud. 1985. *The analysis of defense.* New York: Int. Univ. Press.

Sandler, J., and A.-M. Sandler. 1984. The past unconscious, the present unconscious, and interpretation of the transference. *Psychoanal. Inq.* 4:367–99.

Schafer, R. 1997. *The contemporary Kleinians of London.* Madison, CT: Int. Univ. Press.

Schmidt-Hellerau, C. 2001. *Libido and Lethe. A formalized consistent model of psychoanalytic drive and structure theory.* New York: Other Press.

Schneider, A. Z., and H. Desmond. 1994. The psychoanalytic lawsuit: Expanding opportunities and psychoanalytic training and practice. In *A history of the division of psychoanalysis of the American Psychological Association*, ed. Robert C. Lane and Murray Meisels, 313–35. Hillsdale, NJ: Lawrence Erlbaum Associates.

Scull, A. 2005. Review *The lobotomist: A maverick medical genius and his tragic quest to rid the world of mental illness*, by J. El-Hai. *Los Angeles Times*, Apr. 24.

Shevrin, H. 2003. The consequences of abandoning a comprehensive psychoanalytic theory: Revisiting Rapaport's systematizing attempt. *J. Amer. Psychoanal. Assn.* 51:1005–20.

Smith, H. F. 2005. Dialogues on conflict: Toward an integration of methods. *Psychoanal. Q.* 64:327–63.

Stone, L. 1954. The widening scope of indications for psychoanalysis. *J. Amer. Psychoanal. Assn.* 2:567–94.

———. 1979. Psychoanalysis and psychotherapy, 1954–79. Read at Symposium on Psychoanalysis and Psychotherapy: Twenty-five Years Later, Atlanta, October 20.

Sullivan, H. S. 1953. *The interpersonal theory of psychiatry*. New York: Norton.

Thompson, C. 1950. *Psychoanalysis: Evolution and development*. New York: Hermitage House.

Vanggaard, T. 1968. Contribution to symposium on acting out. *Int. J. Psycho-Anal.* 49:206–10.

Waelder, R. 1960. *Basic theory of neurosis*. New York: Int. Univ. Press.

———. 1962. Psychoanalysis, scientific method, and philosophy. *J. Amer. Psychoanal. Assn.* 10:617–37.

———. 1967. *Progress and revolution*. New York: Int. Univ. Press.

Wallerstein, R. S. 1986. *Forty-two lives in treatment: A study of psychoanalysis and psychotherapy*. New York: Guilford.

———. 1988. One psychoanalysis or many? *Int. J. Psycho-Anal.* 69:5–21.

———. 1991. *The common ground of psychoanalysis*. Northvale, NJ: Aronson.

———. 1998. The IPA and the American Psychoanalytic Association: A perspective on the Regional Association agreement. *Int. J. Psycho-Anal.* 79:553–64.

. 1999. Commentary by Robert S. Wallerstein. To Janine Puget book review of *Politique de la Psychanalyse Face a La Dictature et a La Torture: N'en Parlez a Personne*, by Helena Besserman Vianna. *J. Amer. Psychoanal. Assn.* 47:965–73.

———. 2000. The trajectory of psychoanalysis: Past and future. *Samiksa* 54:17–28.

——— 2003 Politics, science and psychoanalytic history. *J. Amer. Psychoanal. Assn.* 51:7–21.

———. 2005. Dialogue or illusion? How do we go from here? Response to Andre Green. *Int. J. Psycho-Anal.* 86:633–38.

Zilboorg, G. 1941. *A history of medical psychology*. New York: Norton.

INDEX

ABOUT THE AUTHOR

Leo Rangell, MD, has contributed more than 450 articles and seven books to psychoanalytic literature. He has also twice been president of both the American and the International Psychoanalytic Associations. He is currently the honorary president of the International Psychoanalytic Association.